DIGITAL CONVERGENCE

HOW THE MERGING OF COMPUTERS, COMMUNICATIONS, AND MULTIMEDIA IS TRANSFORMING OUR LIVES

by

ANDY COVELL

Illustrations
by
Fredrick Whyte

Aegis Publishing Group, Ltd.
796 Aquidneck Avenue
Newport, Rhode Island
401-849-4200
www.aegisbooks.com

Aegis Publishing Group, Ltd.
796 Aquidneck Avenue
Newport, RI 02842

International Standard Book Number: 1-890154-16-4

Printed in the United States of America.

10 9 8 7 6 5 4 3 2

Library of Congress Cataloging-In-Publication Data:

Covell, Andy.
    Digital convergence : how the merging of computers, communications, and multimedia is transforming our lives / by Andy Covell.
        p.   cm.
    ISBN 1-890154-16-4
    1. Technological innovations—Economic aspects.   2. Technological innovations—Social aspects.   I. Title.
    HC79.T4C69   1999
    332.48'3—dc21   99-37431
                                                        CIP

TABLE OF CONTENTS

INTRODUCTION

Let's begin by exploring the increasing importance of new technologies and introducing the emerging technological phenomenon of digital convergence—what it is, why it's important, and what it can mean to you.

Things are looking up. The economy is humming along at a steady pace, and most of us who want to work have jobs. Stock market run-ups have made millionaires of many average working stiffs. We've got sixty channels on cable, there's an ATM in every mall, and our automobiles are safer than ever. Cigarette use and driving drunk are out, while family values are in, and life expectancy is steadily increasing. Maybe we do live in the best of times.

Life is still fraught with stress and frustration for some of us, of course. The gap between rich and poor widens, and downsizing has forced many from well-paying industrial and corporate jobs to lower-paying service jobs. Working-parent and single-parent lifestyles have made raising a family harder than ever before. Our society continues the struggle to eliminate racism with only marginal success, violence is an issue at every level of society, and so on. Even if these are the best of times, huge challenges remain that we must face both collectively and as individuals.

We are all touched by digital technology in this era, and all but the most Luddite among us can credit technology with some positive impact on important aspects of our business and personal lives. But merely ascribing positive impact to digital technology doesn't do it justice. The evolution of this technology has emerged as a propelling mega-force, regularly spitting out innovative new tools that enable us to address personal, societal, and economic challenges.

In a career of close to twenty years, mostly in higher education, I've had plenty of experience making new technology work for individuals, departments, and large organizations. I am currently director of information technology at the Syracuse University School of Management. This latest experience has been my most interesting one to date, due to recent twists in the evolution of new technology. These developments will be the focus of this book.

When it comes to big-picture social and economic impact, I firmly believe that new technology is the leading force of the day. Some of you may claim that another trend—maybe the increasingly entrepreneurial business climate, the emerging global economy, or the apparent triumph of democratic and free-market principles over communism—is the dominant force. But I submit that new technology clearly has the edge if we consider the impact not only from a global, societal, or macroeconomic view, but also from a view that encompasses the opportunities technology affords the average citizen of the industrialized world.

On a personal level, we've found that new technologies—such as the World Wide Web, Internet email, and videoconferencing—are now used routinely in our workplaces, our homes, or both. These and a variety of other new digital technologies and applications are proving themselves to be powerful tools for communicating, learning, sharing information, entertaining, and conducting business.

Stepping back to take a broader view of things, it is clear that the most prominent societal and economic changes we are now experiencing are intimately tied to technological developments.

For example, the emerging global economy is driven largely by digital technologies—computer networks, digital phone networks, digital video networks, and the Internet—that have dramatically reduced the dimensions of the world.

These technologies overcome the barriers of time and space, thereby turning the entire globe into a ripe marketplace for all manner of goods and services.

Digital technologies also empower entrepreneurs, strengthening a global shift toward a more entrepreneurial business model. Fast-growing, entrepreneurial, high-technology companies are an increasingly important segment of our economy. The meteoric rise in valuation of high-tech stocks has been stunning. Microsoft, Cisco, Broadcast.com, America Online, Intel, and Amazon.com are certainly among the more interesting stories the financial markets have seen over the past few years.

New digital technologies have also leveled the playing field in many low-tech industries and markets. Now, large stodgy corporations, used to having an edge because of their size, find themselves at a disadvantage. They haven't adequately empowered and stimulated employees at all levels to respond to the pace of change and the inherent opportunities of rapid technological evolution. Smaller, leaner, and nimbler entrepreneurial enterprises can more quickly leverage new technology, beating the larger corporations to innovations and opportunities in the marketplace.

These are just a few examples of the impact of new technology. There are many others from all sectors of our society and economy. In my business of higher education, the impact is surely significant and growing, and you'll learn more about the promise and reality of new technology in the university environment as you read further.

Major changes in our society and economy are being shaped by new technology, providing for some fascinating drama during this period of time on earth. But the focus of this book is not the larger social and economic issues. It is my intention to focus on the potential opportunities that new technology will offer individuals.

New digital technologies provide many answers to the question people have asked themselves for generations: "What can I do to get ahead?" It is this aspect of the new technology that is most important to many of you. This book will help you get a better handle on the way today's new digital technologies can empower you to succeed in your work, your business, and your career.

THE EVOLUTION OF DIGITAL TECHNOLOGIES

Digital technologies have evolved at a continuously accelerating pace for the past several decades. But over the last few years there has been a fundamental change in the nature of this evolution—a shift that brings the impact of new digital technologies closer to our lives than ever before.

It undoubtedly occurs to many of you that we've been in the midst of the "computer age" and the "information revolution" for a good twenty years now. What's so new and different? The difference is that digital technology is now being applied to enhance and extend *human interaction*.

My introduction to the incredible power of this new evolutionary thrust occurred when I experienced my first real-time multimedia human interaction via the Internet.

The year was 1994. I had downloaded and installed a free videoconferencing software package developed at Cornell University called CU-SeeMe. This is a videoconferencing system that runs over the Internet. You use it to connect to what's called a reflector, which is a bit like a video chat room. Once connected to the reflector, you see the video images and hear the audio of all the other folks who have connected to the reflector. In turn, they can all see and hear you.

So I hooked up a camera and a microphone, fired up CU-SeeMe, and connected to a reflector somewhere. Only one other person was connected with me. I peered into the screen to get a closer look at him. He peered back. I didn't have my audio working, so he couldn't talk to me. It was my first time, and he apparently realized that I didn't quite get it.

I peered at him again and again, and he peered back. He smiled. Then it began to really sink in—he could see me! I had been using computers for fifteen years, and I had never before communicated with someone this way in real time. Even though I knew what I was getting into, actually being there really stunned me.

My videoconference partner, who looked to be a college-aged dude, seemed quite taken with my reaction. When I realized we were in contact, and he realized that I was stunned, he immediately did a complete 360 degree spin in his swivel chair, waving double peace signs as if to say, "Yaaahoooo! You got it, bud!"

I'll never forget that feeling, that moment.

Within a year we had our first classroom experiment with CU-SeeMe as part of an M.B.A. innovation management course. For a couple of hours each Tuesday, marketing students in Syracuse would discuss research and writings in innovation with a group of engineering students from the University of Waterloo, Canada, and a class of computer science students from the IETSM, a university in Monterrey, Mexico. CU-SeeMe provided an interactive video link for the three groups, a regular conference call speakerphone setup handled the audio, and a Web site enabled faculty and students to share course materials during class sessions.

This approach was fairly crude, but it worked pretty darn well. In addition, it was almost free to us. The CU-SeeMe software was free, Professor Paul Guild at Waterloo created and maintained the Web site, and the other sites placed long distance phone calls to us. We ran the reflector software and bridged the three telephone calls using a standard feature of the University's phone system.

While there were some minor glitches, it was a clear success. The class not only brought three disciplines together, but it also brought together students from three different economies and cultures, creating an exciting mix of ideas. The North American Free Trade Agreement (NAFTA) had recently come into being, further heightening the relevance of class discussions.

New developments in digital technology, such as Internet videoconferencing, facilitate human interaction and are now reshaping how we learn, how we conduct business, and how we entertain ourselves. The overall impact of these new technologies is consistent with the impact of other technologies—such as the printing press, the telephone, and the television—that have fundamentally altered the ability of humans to communicate, interact, and share information.

Before we focus any further on what's happening with today's technology, let's take a quick look back at earlier phases of digital technology evolution.

THE DAWN OF COMPUTING

For the first few decades of the digital revolution, technology was applied in ways that were very productive, but not all that noticeable in our everyday lives. Digital electronic computers were first developed to assist in numerical calculation. While the impact of early digital technologies on our lives was limited, these computers did have an important role. For example:

- They allowed the government to more efficiently perform the decennial census, and to analyze that data to develop new policies.
- They were central to NASA's space exploration efforts.
- In the corporate sector, advanced R&D projects leveraged this computational resource to develop useful products.
- In our universities, computers were used for cutting-edge research in hard and social sciences.

My only recollections of these computers during my early childhood were the reports of computer-simulated boxing matches that I would hear about on my old AM radio. It wasn't until the seventh grade that I saw my first real live computer device. It was a key punch at Clarkson College of Technology (now Clarkson University), one of two colleges in my small home town in upstate New York. It was pretty cool and it impressed me as futuristic, but it wasn't even a full-fledged computer.

By the time I saw or used a real computer, I was in

high school. In an advanced chemistry class, again at Clarkson College, I had the opportunity to use a minicomputer. I vividly recall watching the print ball spin and whir as it typed out messages from the computer's "brain." What a thrill!

Other than those early experiences, the only computers I ever saw on a regular basis were the ones with lots of blinking lights that I'd see in the movies or on television. That sort of unrealistic exposure to computing was typical. Many of the people I knew while growing up in the '60s and early '70s never had occasion to see a "real" computer.

THE MAINFRAME ERA

Over time, computers evolved into useful tools for automating business recordkeeping tasks and managing business information. During this era, the large mainframe computers that handled these chores eventually came to dominate the computing landscape.

In the 1970s, we began to see the impact of these mainframe computers as they managed, manipulated, and analyzed large amounts of information and automated the functions of millions of knowledge workers in all sorts of organizations.

We began to see evidence of these increasingly important digital technologies in everyday life when:

- We visited the department of motor vehicles, and a clerk typed our information into a green screen CRT tube.
- We received a utility bill or a college grade report that had been printed on a mainframe printer.
- We were given computer-generated paycheck stubs for pay that was electronically deposited into our checking accounts.

Corporate leaders of the day understood that mainframe computers enabled large organizations to automate functions and manage information effectively, thereby facilitating high-volume manufacturing, inventory control, distribution, and sales. This capacity for managing and coordinating a high volume of business stimulated the growth of big business, creating a golden era for corporations.

It was a golden era of sorts for those of us in the information technology (IT) business, too. Mainframe computing required huge corporate financial outlays for central equipment and a significant centralized technical staff.

I spent a decade in the 1980s as a mainframe programmer, systems analyst, and database administrator. I experienced firsthand the combination of mainframe-based automation, information management, and organizational connectedness that led to some extremely useful applications. At Syracuse University, this was exemplified by our library automation/card catalog system, student record system, and general ledger and payroll processing systems.

The mainframe era was also a time for empire building among corporate IT executives. This resulted in what many corporate users felt was too much bureaucracy, leaving them with too little control over information systems and technology. It was also during this era that an ugly "attitude" developed among many central IT staff toward mainframe "users"—a condescending tone and body language that even today makes my hair stand up on the back of my neck. Sadly, I still encounter that attitude on occasion when dealing with central and departmental IT professionals.

POWER TO THE PC

With the advent of the personal computer in the 1980s, a new era of using the computer as a productivity tool was launched. Easy-to-use and highly functional word processing, spreadsheet, and database programs provided a platform of functionality that allowed individuals, workgroups, and small organizations to increase productivity. When starting a business, organizing a Little League, managing sales contact information, or writing a book, we could leverage this tool to help us work more efficiently and effectively.

The power of the PC was not relegated to large organizations. It was a tool for people working at the grass roots level. Whether that was in a small department of a large corporation, a small business, or a home office, the PC was a tool that could help anyone who needed to organize, track, or analyze information efficiently.

From my point of view, the personal computer was a marginal tool for many years. The old Commodore computer my family purchased was a total bomb as far as I was concerned, and the IBM-compatible computers I tried offered no clear advantage. When compared to the mainframe I had access to, I could perform all the functions of the PC, only faster, whether word processing, analyzing data, or managing a database. Plus, I could plug into the mainframe via modem from anywhere in the world. I could also create applications that anyone in the university would be able to access from a mainframe terminal.

Of course, I was trained as a computer programmer. Less fortunate souls had to submit their mainframe system requests to a management information systems (MIS) group, where the request was placed in a queue. In those days, the backlog of outstanding requests in the MIS queue was infamous in most programming shops, providing a constant source of discussion among "users" at the office water cooler.

It wasn't until I used my first Macintosh that I felt a PC offered something more than what I had on the mainframe. What was the big attraction? Its icons and mouse? No. For me, it was the ability to edit a document that appeared on-screen almost exactly as it would look when printed, and to print that document in near pub-

lication quality on a laser printer. At the time, this was nearly impossible on either a mainframe or an IBM PC.

For many people, the personal computer (IBM-compatible PC or Macintosh) was an opportunity to take control of information and boost productivity. No more waiting for the MIS group to program a simple information system. No more tedious typewriter or pen-and-ink efforts to create and edit documents or maintain the business books. Once the PC reached a standard, relatively inexpensive, and fairly usable configuration in the 1980s, the PC revolution hit full stride.

The advent of PC networks furthered the PC revolution. The PC grew from a stand-alone tool to an enterprise communications device. Networked PC users could easily share information within the workgroup or across the corporate enterprise, as well as share peripheral devices such as printers.

This ability to share information and interact electronically was a forerunner to the current era of digital convergence. However, small organizations and individuals were not networked, and there was no common infrastructure for interconnecting the islands of connectivity: consumer desktops, small office LANs, and huge corporate networks. Communication and interaction was limited almost exclusively to text and numbers. Corporate uses of computer-based communication tools remained focused on internal productivity and information sharing.

Digital Convergence

A whole new era is now beginning as digital convergence technologies and applications enhance human experience and organizational function in exciting new ways.

In the past few years, the capability of all types of computing devices—from the handheld computer to the largest supercomputer— has dramatically increased. The typical desktop computer, now in millions of homes and on every businessman's desk, has a very fast processor, large disk drive, and lightning-fast input/output operations.

During the time that the desktop computer has matured, a variety of specialized digital tools has emerged for capturing, manipulating, and combining different kinds of media. The resulting media experience—featuring a combination of audio, image, text, and video—is known as multimedia.

The ability to create multimedia content and to deliver a multimedia experience differentiates the PC from other consumer electronics devices such as a stereo sound system or a television. The desktop computer is clearly at the center of the multimedia experience, and the evolution of digital media capabilities and the growth in digital content over the past several years has been stunning.

As computing and computer-based multimedia technologies have evolved, so too have communications technologies. We have witnessed dramatic improvements in speed, capacity, and the ability to support digital communication in these technologies.

Digital computer networks enable data transmission among personal computers and between PCs and large server computers. These networks provide shared functions and information over dedicated local area and wide area corporate networks, dial-up modems connected to old analog phone lines, public digital phone lines, and public computer networks such as the Internet. Increasingly, other digital devices, such as handheld computers and television set-top boxes are also connected via the digital network communications infrastructure.

Digital convergence is the merging of these improved computing capabilities, new digital multimedia technologies and content, and new digital communications technologies. This combination of computing power and functionality, digital networked interconnectedness, and multimedia capability enables new forms of human interaction, collaboration, and information sharing.

While we'll explore several digital convergence technologies and applications in detail in Chapter 7, let's get a taste for what's out there before leaving this chapter. As we work through the next five chapters to build a foundation of knowledge of the underlying technologies, it will be important to have some notion of what digital convergence technologies and their capabilities are. I've already mentioned a few of these technologies, but let me take a moment to offer a brief description of some of the more prominent ones to give you a mental picture of the sorts of digital convergence technologies available now.

Email (a.k.a. electronic mail) enables the sending and receipt of electronic messages between individuals and among groups. While earlier incarnations of email allowed for only plain-text messages, new email systems enable messages that can include images and rich text (text with variable fonts, colors, tables, and so on). Most modern email systems also allow for the inclusion of email attachments such as spreadsheets, presentations, documents, or other electronic files that can accompany an email message. Some advanced email systems support voice messages and even video messages. Of course, any system worth its salt adheres to standards that ensure your email can be exchanged throughout the global Internet.

The **World Wide Web**, probably the most compelling digital convergence technology, provides a user-friendly graphical interface to multimedia resources stored on Internet-accessible World Wide Web servers. The user's program, called a Web browser, lets the user retrieve a variety of media and interact with remote computers through electronic forms that enable data entry. The two most popular Web browsers are Microsoft Internet Explorer and Netscape Navigator.

While many Web sites are set up and run by large corporations and professional Web design teams, many other Web sites are set up and maintained by regular folks. All you need are some good ideas, a little knowledge of how to develop Web pages using HyperText Markup Language (HTML, the computer language of the Web), and the resources to rent space on a Web server or to set one up from scratch. The Web has hit the mainstream, and it is currently the dominant digital convergence technology.

Videoconferencing allows us to experience interactive sound and video between two geographically disparate locations, or among several locations. During a videoconference, a remote location appears to be an extension of the local environment that we view through the "window" of the videoconferencing system.

Videoconferencing systems come in a wide range of price and quality combinations. Some videoconferencing

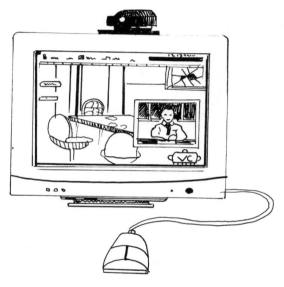

systems connect users on corporate computer or telecommunication networks; some connect via analog phone lines; some connect over high-speed digital phone lines; and some use the Internet.

Internet streaming audio and video technologies deliver audio and video feeds, in real time or on demand, across the Internet. Digital audio and video media is transmitted from a media server on the Internet to an Internet-connected PC. Then the video is projected on the monitor, and the audio is delivered through the computer's speakers.

The quality of both audio and video tends to be somewhat mediocre due to the current performance characteristics and limitations of the Internet. But the ability to easily deliver audio and video anywhere on the Internet is quite potent, and this technology has tremendous potential.

DIGITAL CONVERGENCE AND YOU

Prior digital eras focused on calculation, automation, information management, and personal productivity. Digital convergence technologies possess characteristics that combine to set this era apart. From a technical standpoint, the power of digital convergence rests on the ability to:

- ◆ represent audio, video, text, images, and other media in digital form;
- ◆ easily manage, edit, integrate, and transmit this digital content; and
- ◆ tie this rich media to interactive services and transactional capability.

The remaining chapters detail this incredible technological phenomenon. However, in an effort to help you place this emerging technological trend within the context of your own life and career, I want to highlight the important ways in which digital convergence impacts human reality.

HUMAN INTERACTION

First and foremost, you must recognize that we are not discussing humanoids staring blankly at computer screens. Rather, the desktop computer serves as a communications tool that enables humans to touch the lives, the work, the hearts, and the pocketbooks of other humans. From chat rooms to Internet telephony, digital convergence technologies and applications facilitate human interaction and collaboration like no other technologies that have come before.

Recently, there was a sad news item here in central New York. A 50-something small-town wife discovered the Internet and struck up a relationship with a male cyber-companion. Her husband got wind of this, became very upset, and ended up stabbing her in the neck. I saw her on the news, and she appeared to have weathered the attack. She asked to have the charges against her husband dropped, but that won't happen. This is a sad story, but a story that illustrates the power of this new technology to bring people together—and to tear them apart as well.

The human desire to connect with a community of like-minded people provides another example. The connectivity and media-handling capabilities of digital convergence technologies provide new opportunities to seek out and interact with people who really interest us, and possibly learn from them or conduct business with them.

For most of us, community is defined by the people we interact with near our homes, in our workplaces, at our professional conferences and meetings, and in our places of worship. Now, new technologies have created electronic communities, often dubbed virtual communities, that defy geographic barriers. These are not pretend communities. They foster the same close human interaction, sharing, and caring that is characteristic of traditional communities. They are diverse communities as well: communities of coworkers in large, far-flung corporations; global communities of special-interest groups; communities derived from professional organizations; communities that focus on common recreational pursuits; and communities that share a common purpose.

This ability to create and build community has already begun to benefit us all as groups of scientists, engineers, medical professionals, and educators have been able to organize and interact, making significant progress on many important issues and initiatives. However, the results are not uniformly positive or upbeat. Much has been written and said about electronic communities at the margins. Some of these communities, such as hate groups or the militia movement, have built significant ill will that has led to destructive or harmful activity.

As I write this, a white supremacist in Texas has just been sentenced to death for the brutal killing of a black man, and the Southern Poverty Law Center reports that the Internet has empowered the white supremacist community. Of course it has. It empowers all geographically dispersed special-interest communities. But I have no doubt that technology has also empowered many communities that contribute positively to our society and to our growth as a species.

If you aren't already interacting with a virtual community, there will be a point in the future when you will want or need to interact electronically with a group of people that shares an interest or an idea of yours. These folks won't work and live anywhere near you, won't go to your church, and won't work for your company, but they may very well end up having a significant impact on your life.

APPEAL

Digital convergence programs and interfaces often include attractive graphics, richly formatted textual material, audio, and video. People who were turned off when using older versions of WordPerfect, DBASE, Telnet, and FTP have quickly warmed to today's rich and user-friendly personal computer that offers an attractive and multimedia-enabled interface.

The incredible growth of the World Wide Web illustrates the power of this appeal. I've been an Internet user since the mid-1980s. But I didn't have a lot of company for the first several years because Internet use was limited almost exclusively to academia, and corporate or government research departments. In the early 1990s, the World Wide Web was invented, and it was quickly adapted to support graphics and helper programs that made surfing the Web a multimedia experience. Once that happened, interest in and adoption of the Internet took off like wildfire!

I remember well the rush to get on the Web. I still get a tickle when the Giants kick an extra point against the hated Cowboys, and through the uprights you see:

www.dallascowboys.com

OPPORTUNITIES

Digital convergence technologies and applications comprise a very rich set of facilities that can be deployed in more settings and for a wider range of purposes than earlier mainstream digital technologies. Let's focus on a particular venue, the elementary classroom, to illustrate the breadth of opportunity provided by digital convergence technologies.

When automation and information management were the main applications of digital technology, elementary teachers and students had relatively little use for the technology. Library catalogs, recordkeeping (grades), and ordering tasks were all gradually turned over to mainframes and minicomputers, but day-to-day classroom learning was not significantly touched during this era.

Computers made their way into the classroom when personal computing emerged. Teachers and students used stand-alone software to administer the classroom and to reinforce classroom instruction with educational games and drill programs such as the Oregon Trail, Number Munchers, and The Marketplace. During this phase, the computer became an important classroom tool, but its use was limited.

Community and government support for funding technology in elementary education was present, but spotty.

Now, with digital convergence offering a broad array of instructional experiences for students—highlighted by rich communication, collaboration, and information access tools that focus primarily on the Internet and the World Wide Web—computers are being integrated into the activities of the elementary classroom like never before. Students can engage in real-time learning opportunities across the globe via videoconferencing. They can share ideas with students from other countries and cultures via email, and they can tell the world about their communities and themselves with classroom and personal Web pages. These are obvious examples of valuable learning experiences.

Fortunately, community and government support for wiring and equipping elementary classrooms is at an all-time high. The broader, deeper impact of digital technologies is a theme being played out in all industries and organizations.

EMPOWERING INDIVIDUALS, ENTREPRENEURS, AND CORPORATE WORKGROUPS

In prior phases of the evolution of digital technologies, users were constrained to a relatively limited set of technology functions and capabilities. Many of the most important technological applications were left entirely to a professional MIS staff or external consultants.

The new era of digital convergence offers a much wider scope of opportunity and, at the same time, provides more accessible capability. This combination rewards a growing number of savvy users who can let their creative juices flow. These users have proven their ability to identify and exploit new technologies, but they also know that sometimes the assistance of a person with specialized technical skills and expertise is required, whether a part-time high school geek or an MIS professional.

Certainly entrepreneurs will continue to gain an advantage over stagnant, overly bureaucratic corporations. While the corporation as a whole can benefit from digital convergence, corporate entrepreneurs and workgroups are particularly empowered by the new technology. Innovative corporate uses of technology will tend to bubble up from the trenches rather than result from decisions made by the corporate brass or plans developed and implemented by a central MIS staff.

I've spent most of my career in higher education, but I did have one stint at a fairly large health insurance company. Here, I experienced a stodgy culture where innovation was regularly suppressed. I was known for my interest in PCs, networks, and other related technologies. As a result, I was frequently approached by corporate managers and workers who were frustrated by the mainframe orientation of the central MIS group and the lack of support for desktop and departmental computing. The corporate MIS group had even gotten approval to acquire and deploy a mainframe version of WordPerfect to nip the growing demand for desktop PCs in the bud.

I was manager of research and development, and I wanted to use PCs to deliver the results of our analyses in a more useful format that would complement the raw numbers. This might include nicely formatted tables, graphs, and figures, but some of my biggest customers didn't want that. These top-level executives had been in the company for many decades, rising up through the ranks, and they wanted to keep their mainframe reports unchanged, complete with page after page of numbers printed by 132-character-wide impact printers on green bar paper. Needless to say, I had trouble getting support to buy new PCs that would enhance our reporting functions.

In other departments, workers saw a slew of ways to leverage personal computer technology, but they too were often stymied in their efforts by a lack of managerial support and a lack of funds for technology purchases. An interesting corporate sport developed as a result of this situation. The ongoing game was to develop schemes to secure funding for desktop computers and then tie these computers together in a rogue network. Middle managers like myself were constantly coming up with new strategies, comparing notes, and commiserating over failed efforts.

Eventually, the corporate brain trust realized that PCs and networks were good for the company. But by that time, I had left.

Corporate reluctance to adopt and deploy new technology is a story I've heard repeated many times while working with and teaching business professionals. They tell me of disabled CD-ROM drives, bans on modems, PCs locked down so that a piece of software can't be installed without the help of an MIS systems programmer, severe restrictions on Internet use and access, and purchase policies that prohibit including a sound card in a new PC purchase order.

The negative consequences of this pattern are increasing as digital convergence technologies offer ever greater opportunities for stimulating new business and enhancing internal operations and effectiveness. Savvy corporate leaders will recognize that new technology empowers individuals and workgroups, and they will move to eliminate stifling bureaucracies, policies, and cultural barriers.

SUCCESS STORIES

Let's check out some real-life success stories that exemplify the benefit of these new technologies. These are not the sort of high-profile examples that you've read about in *Newsweek* or *Time* or seen profiled on the *CBS Evening News*. There is no Matt Drudge story here. These are people like you and me who are leveraging new technology to add value to whatever it is they work on, or pursue, for love or money, or both. With these simple examples, you will begin to see the potential of digital convergence technologies at both an individual and an organizational level.

Research Collaboration

With Microsoft NetMeeting, two computers equipped with standard sound cards and microphones can establish audio communications across the Internet, thus enabling the individuals who use those computers to engage in a conversation. The cost to conference this way across the globe via the Internet is the cost of the local connection to the Internet. Considerable amounts can be saved on long-distance fees, depending on who it is you talk to on a regular basis.

Another great feature of conferencing with NetMeeting is the ability to share documents and files while you're talking. You can pull up a spreadsheet or presentation during your discussion and make modifications to it as you speak.

I recently helped Alex Thevaranjan, an accounting professor, use Microsoft NetMeeting to discuss joint research with a colleague at Ohio State University. He saved the University a ton on long-distance charges, and, while he was talking, he could pull up and share tables, diagrams, and text. Although not an earth-shattering application, NetMeeting did help Professor Thevaranjan move his research forward, which is critically important for an untenured faculty member at a research university.

Collecting Simpsons!

Bill LaRue is a television critic for the Syracuse Newspapers. He's also a Simpsons fan and has developed a fondness for collecting Simpsons toys and other Simpsons merchandise. In 1996, he decided that a Web site would be a good way to get in touch with other Simpsons collectors, so he launched his Collecting Simpsons! Web site. (You can check it out at *http://members.aol.com/bartfan.*)

He accomplished his goal of getting in touch with Simpsons collectors—lots of Simpsons collectors. Bill also discovered that he can generate additional income by participating in the associate programs of electronic commerce sites. Such sites included Amazon.com (selling books, CDs, and other stuff on the Web) and eToys.com (selling toys in cyberspace).

To participate, he provides links on his Web pages to these e-commerce sites or to specific products at the site. If people click through and purchase, he gets a return of 5 to 15 percent of the total sale. His site is now funneling thousands of dollars in business to eToys.com and Amazon.com every quarter, and Bill is enjoying a significant return on that business.

Bill is exploring the prospects for launching a site with a broader appeal, covering several lines of toys rather than just Simpsons merchandise. Though he loves his job at the newspaper, he now thinks that he could garner enough extra income to make a reasonable living via the right Web site.

Sassy Scrubs

Sometimes you need to secure special technical expertise to leverage digital convergence technology. Peggy

Piontkowski is the owner of Sassy Scrubs, a small company that makes surgical scrubs. She has been an innovator in this industry by bringing out scrubs that use new patterns and materials, and her young venture has met with great success. Her scrubs have even been picked up by the NBC hit television show *E.R.*

She started her business in her home by taking orders over the phone. Eventually she opened a storefront to sell her merchandise, and she was recently set to expand her floor space with the purchase of a 5,000-square-foot building. But the Web called.

She had been mulling over how she could take maximum advantage of the Web. Most everyone she talked to suggested setting up a site to promote her merchandise with no direct selling. "What's the point?" she thought to herself. Then she met Gene and Cathy Wolf, Syracuse-based Web consultants. They sold her on the idea of a full e-commerce site that would handle online sales using DXShop, an Internet e-commerce tool that their firm deploys on a regular basis.

The first week that *http://www.sassyscrubs.com* was online, it made $500 in sales with zero promotion of the site. Search-engine hits alone were enough to generate significant traffic, resulting in an opening week sales volume that greatly exceeded expectations. Peggy also noted that the average amount of a Web-based sale was double the average sale at either her store or over the phone.

Peggy is sold on this new vehicle for selling Sassy Scrubs, and her plans to purchase a new building are on hold indefinitely.

OVERCOME THE BARRIERS AND KICK SOME BUTT!

While digital convergence is truly a bright light, holding great promise for each and every one of us, it does have its pitfalls and drawbacks. There is the rash of "amazing" technology developments, the profusion of new products, the complexity and unreliability of many new technologies, and the misleading media and vendor hype. All this leaves many overwhelmed and untrusting of the new technology.

Then there are the many other technological, social, political, and economic barriers that hinder the evolution and widespread acceptance of new technology based on digital convergence. Such barriers include Internet performance problems, security and privacy issues, telecommunications regulations, and desktop processing requirements for high-quality media playback. These are just a few of the issues and challenges that you'll need to know about to make sense of the evolution of digital convergence and to act on the opportunities that can make it exciting and worthwhile for you.

Given the problems, realities, and issues, many people are quickly turned off. This is unfortunate. Digital convergence technologies, when properly deployed, can truly enhance the functions and communications of both humans and organizations in ways that are not only tolerable, but actually quite pleasant, reliable, and productive.

Anyone with smarts and initiative can chart a course through the rough technological waters to identify and implement solutions that will bring value to an individual and his or her enterprise. It may not be easy, and there are aspects of this activity that will require a trained pro. But the intellectual process of identifying your needs and opportunities and then matching them up with available technologies is something that you can and should consider. When done properly, this is an activity that will reap valuable rewards and lead to personal success.

Between downsizing and the rise of the entrepreneur, you may now find yourself in a smaller, leaner, meaner organization that is struggling to outdo the outfit across town or the outfit in your vertical market across the globe. It has gotten harder than ever for many of us to elevate our games, so to speak, in a way that really lets us say, "Hey, I can kick some butt here!"

Digital convergence technologies offer you an opportunity to gain a competitive advantage that can put you and your organization ahead. If you get behind the technology thrust and really make digital convergence opportunities fly in your setting, you can contribute in a way that will make a huge difference, getting your light out from under the barrel in the process.

My goal is to help you along that path. This book seeks to demystify digital convergence, guiding you through the technology concepts and issues that may overwhelm or frustrate you. It also provides a good dose of reality therapy along the way. By offering valuable background information, it will stimulate you to think through many technological issues as they apply to you, depending on your position in life and your personal goals and objectives.

This book will instill in you a framework of understanding—a synthesis of information, analyses, and insights—that will provide an effective starting point for exploring digital convergence opportunities further. It will fill you in on technologies, technological trends, and implementation issues so you will have a balanced understanding of digital convergence. This is something that is not easily grasped from reading focused magazine articles, vendor white papers, books that focus on specific technologies, or volumes that offer a 50,000-mile-high executive view of technology and its impact on our society and economy.

Of course, this is not a detailed and exhaustive technological treatise. For many of you, it may be a first step. You'll need to follow up with additional technical research, training, and some hands-on learning if you wish to take that next step toward technological empowerment. You'll find some useful suggestions as to where and how you can learn more about digital convergence technologies and applications in Chapter 8.

If this book helps some of you learn how to navigate the technological landscape without fear, so that you can launch an effort to employ technology effectively and reap the rewards of that effort, then it will be a success. If it helps some of you better understand what's happening around you, just so you can cope a little more effectively, it will have served its purpose also.

However, this book is not solely for those of you who are technologically intimidated or underinformed. This book is also for those of you who are actively using new technologies, but want to better understand the transformations occurring as the technology evolves at an ever increasing pace. You will find insights, tips, and advice that are useful not only to the technophobes trying to make a new start, but also to the techno-savvy warriors in the trenches, slogging away at the front lines of innovation. Parts of the technology overview material may be old hat for this group, but many of the issues and ideas presented will stimulate fresh and productive thinking.

2 CONVENTIONAL TECHNOLOGIES

So you want to leverage the power of new digital convergence technologies? To easily and accurately recognize opportunities to deploy these new technologies, you must first gain an understanding of and appreciation for the conventional communications and information-sharing technologies.

Digital convergence technologies are exciting because they provide new ways to facilitate human interaction. In the absence of digital convergence, such interactions are carried out in face-to-face meetings, on the telephone, through printed forms and paperwork, or via published sources that include books, magazines, and newspapers. Communication also occurs through a variety of commonplace audio and video media such as motion pictures, radio, broadcast television, audio recordings on cassette tape, and VHS video recordings.

Each conventional communication tool has proven itself at some point from the birth of human language to the electronics era of the past few decades. Most of us have at least some notion of the incredible influence these forms of communication have had on our civilization. The new wave of digital convergence technologies promises a breadth and depth of impact approaching or exceeding that of these earlier human interaction milestones.

In the near term, most digital convergence technologies will complement conventional technologies rather than replace them. To effectively leverage the opportunities of digital convergence, you must come to appreciate and understand conventional technologies, which are so often taken for granted in the digital age. It's also useful to gain some understanding of how these technologies work because new digital convergence technologies have incorporated and adapted many of the technological mechanisms and techniques that were developed for conventional tools.

Combine that knowledge with a solid understanding of digital technologies and their advantages over conventional technologies, and you'll be able to accurately identify when conventional technologies are the most appropriate and when digital convergence technologies and tools offer an edge. Plus, you'll be sure to avoid the trap that many people fall into who spend time and resources pursuing high-tech "solutions" that are ultimately inferior to solutions based on old-fashioned conventional technologies.

WHY ISN'T THIS A WEB SITE?

Some of you may wonder why I've chosen to present a book on digital convergence via the medium of the printed page rather than the Web. This book provides an example of how a conventional technology, the printing press, can be more effective than an alternative digital convergence technology.

The application of any technology that facilitates human interaction and the sharing of information should occur only after a careful analysis of the alternatives. I could have put this content together on a Web site, or I could have put it together as a video on VHS tape, or I could have arranged a television program on a local public-access cable channel.

My purpose is to convey a set of ideas and beliefs along with a body of information and some reasoned analysis. As with any effort at human interaction, an analysis of the alternatives must take into account the purpose of the interaction, the participants, the relative strengths and weaknesses of the candidate technologies, and the context of those technologies. The content I have to share is fairly voluminous (though this isn't *War and Peace*), and I think it should be consumed in an environment conducive to concentration and reflection. Individualized interaction is not required. Eventually some give-and-take may be appropriate between myself and certain participants, but the maximum benefit will be derived if there are many participants, many more than I could interact with on a one-to-one basis.

The top candidate technologies for imparting these ideas and information were the printing press and the World Wide Web. Television probably wouldn't be feasible, and a video tape would reach a very limited audience because I have limited funds for marketing. In addition, I'm camera shy!

Choosing between the book and the Web, I think the book is a winner for a number of reasons:

■ I want to communicate a significant amount of material, and the printed page is an efficient medium for transmitting this content. People can read at a rapid pace, and most people find reading a book much easier on the eyes than reading from a computer screen.

■ Once you've acquired the book, you can consume its content anywhere you choose—on a mountaintop, at your kid's soccer game, on the subway, or in the bathroom. You can be lying down, standing up, or sitting pretty. This flexibility enhances the likelihood that you will consume it in a setting where you're comfortable, allowing you to reflect on what you learn and how you can apply it to your unique situation.

■I've written a great deal over the past couple of decades, and I think I've developed an ability to boil down and explain a complex set of technological concepts in written form (I hope you agree). The book allows me to leverage this skill to develop its content for your use, enabling the sharing of information and advice with a global audience in a comprehensive and timely fashion.

■A rock-solid industry is already established that can print, bind, distribute, and market the book. People in bookstores are actively seeking books that have the content I am writing about. The book allows me to focus on developing this content, leaving the bulk of the marketing and selling to my publisher and his industry.

I hope you get a lot out of this book. I also hope you'll take the time to check out the combination of video, links, community interaction, and additional information that I plan to put together at *http://www.digital-convergence.com.*

Now, let's turn our attention to some of the ingenious, human-engineered manipulations of physical properties upon which conventional technologies—and many digital convergence technologies—are based.

WAVES, ELECTRONS, AND MAGNETISM

WAVES

Each of the conventional technologies incorporates some combination of light and sound waves to get a message from one human being to another. These waves appear to us as written or spoken words, still or moving pictures, or music. More recent conventional technologies, such as television, telephone, and radio, rely on the ingenious use of electricity, electromagnetic waves (which we can't see or hear), and magnetism to extend the reach and timeliness of human communication.

Drop a stone into a calm pool of water and watch the waves ripple from where you dropped the stone to the edges of the pool. The waves you see are a form of energy that moves through the water without moving the water.

Unlike the waves you see in water, most of the waves in our environment (including the waves used in conventional technologies) are invisible to the human eye as individual waves. But they all carry energy the same way the wave on a pond carries energy. While these waves can't all be created and seen as easily as a wave on water, they can be created, detected, manipulated, and measured using special devices such as light bulbs, oscillators, thermometers, lasers, microphones, prisms, and antennas.

Humans sense light waves and sound waves with their eyes and ears, interpreting them as sights and sounds. Sound waves let us listen for geese, hear a fire alarm, talk on the phone, or listen to modern rock. Light allows us to read the newspaper, appreciate a sculpture or a photograph, read a textbook, or watch a tennis match. With light and sound together, we can see a movie, take in a lecture, engage in conversation and check out the body language, or catch a lounge act.

It is sound and light that enable almost all forms of human communication and learning. The conventional technologies we use every day allow us to transmit, store, retrieve, and receive sound and light in ways that greatly enhance our experience on earth.

SOUND

Sound waves are created by anything that can vibrate at a rate of around 2,000 to 15,000 times per second, the audible range of human hearing. The vibration generates the alternating compression and decompression of matter that constitutes a sound wave. Sound waves can be transmitted through any form of matter that can carry these compression waves, including air and water. But  because this wave form travels as compressed and decompressed matter, sound waves cannot travel through empty space (such as a vacuum or outer space). When sound waves reach our ears, they cause our eardrums to vibrate, allowing us to hear.

Whether high-pitched like a bird's song, deep like a fog horn, or somewhere in between, the pitch of a sound is a function of the distance between areas of compression and decompression. It is expressed as a frequency of change between alternating compression and decompression at a fixed point over time. The intensity of the sound, or loudness, is a function of the amplitude of the waves. Amplitude is a fancy word for the difference in intensity between the compression and decompression phases of the vibration.

LIGHT

Light waves are a different kind of wave than sound waves. They are electromagnetic waves (also called rays) made of electric and magnetic energy fields that alternate together over time. Light includes a band of electromagnetic wave frequencies covering the full spectrum of colors we see. The color of light is determined by wave frequency, which is a measurement of how often the electromagnetic wave form passes a fixed point. It is sometimes expressed as a wavelength, which is the distance of one full cycle of the wave as it travels through space. The amplitude of a light wave determines its intensity or brightness.

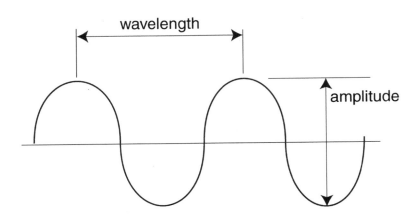

In general, electromagnetic waves have a much greater frequency than sound waves. Electromagnetic wave forms vary on the order of tens of thousands to hundreds of millions of times per second. Also, unlike sound waves, electromagnetic waves can travel through empty space.

We see light (1) by focusing our eyes on a light source such as the sun, a light bulb, a burning match, or a computer monitor, and (2) by viewing light that is reflected off objects and surfaces around us.

Many surfaces absorb light rays, so the light is not reflected. When a surface absorbs light waves from the entire spectrum and white light is shown on it, it looks black. If an object reflects all colors (the full spectrum of light waves), it appears white.

For example, the paper on which these words appear looks white because it doesn't absorb any of the light waves that you have shining on it. They are reflected, allowing you to see it as white paper. On the other hand, the printed words were created using an ink that absorbs all wavelengths of light, so they appear black.

The same phenomenon applies to all other colors you see on any object that is not a light source. So if you have a red car, it is red because it reflects red light waves and absorbs all others. If you shine a yellow bug light on a surface that reflects all light waves, it will appear yellow.

CREATING COLOR

Conventional technologies use two methods to create colors, and the results appear in all conventional media, including television, magazines, books, and billboards.

One method, called color subtraction, is used to create colors with reflected light for media such as color publications or color photography. Color subtraction uses three secondary colors—yellow, magenta, and cyan—and each

secondary color absorbs one of the three primary colors.

When applied to reflective material such as white paper, secondary-colored dyes and inks can be applied in combination to create any color. In printing, black ink is often used to strengthen darker colors and to serve as a single ink source for pure black print areas. Typeface, for example, uses pure black ink, thereby conserving the three colored inks.

To print an image of the red car, we would use a mixture of magenta ink to absorb green light waves and yellow ink to absorb blue light waves. The printed surface now reflects only red light waves.

The other method, called color addition, is used when creating colors that use light sources. This is how a television or computer monitor creates color. Three primary color sources—red, green, and blue—are combined to make all other colors, including white. To project a red car on your television set or computer monitor, a red light source is used with no contribution from the green and blue light sources.

ELECTRONS

Electrons are atomic particles that can move at nearly the speed of light under certain conditions. To produce electricity, the electrons are contained in a material, called a conductor, that frees them to move about, and a voltage is applied. Voltage consists of a positive electron source and a negative electron sink.

One important characteristic of electricity is its ability to increase, decrease, and reverse the flow of electrons by varying the positive source and negative sink. This makes it possible to mimic the behavior of sound waves or the intensity of light waves by regulating the electron flow. The voltage is made to vary over time in the same way that the sound or light waves vary, thus creating an analog of the original sound or light wave. This is known as analog technology, a term you've probably heard before.

Once the original sound or light is converted to an electrical signal, electronic devices are used to modify the electrical flow and adjust the signal as needed. For example, an amplifier increases the intensity of a sound signal so that it is adequate to drive a speaker system. Amplifiers are usually equipped with some sort of dial that lets you control the volume by dynamically altering the electron flow.

ELECTRONS AND MAGNETISM

Another interesting property of electron flow is magnetism. When electrons flow through a circuit, a magnetic field is created around that circuit. The polarity of the magnetism and the strength of the magnetic field can be controlled by altering both the direction

and the rate of electron flow. This property is used to convert an analog sound signal to sound waves. The electrical signal is amplified and then used to create alternating magnetic fields. These fields, in turn, vibrate a speaker cone to generate the sound waves you hear.

RADIO WAVES

There is also a set of electromagnetic wave frequencies, generically referred to as radio waves, that serve as helper waves in the transmission of analog audio and video. Radio waves are used to enable a variety of communications, including AM/ FM radio, shortwave radio, VHF and UHF television, cellular telephone, and satellite communications.

How does this work? A uniform electromagnetic wave form, called a carrier wave, is altered at broadcast time so that variations applied to the standard wave form coincide with an analog electrical signal. The carrier wave is said to be impressed, or imprinted, with the analog signal. When the broadcast wave is received, the changes applied prior to broadcast are extracted to recreate the original analog electrical signal. This signal then drives a speaker or display monitor. Alteration of the carrier wave with analog information is called modulation, and the extraction of the analog signal from the carrier wave at the receiving device is called demodulation.

The alteration of the carrier wave can be an alteration to the frequency of the wave. FM radio works this way (FM standing for frequency modulation). It is also possible to use a wave with a fixed frequency and alter the amplitude. This is known as amplitude modulation (AM) and is used by AM radio.

VHF (very high frequency) and UHF (ultrahigh frequency) waves use modulated signals to carry audio and video to your rooftop antenna (if you happen to have one). The first-generation consumer satellite television systems also use electromagnetic waves to carry analog sound and video signals that are received by a satellite dish. Newer consumer satellite systems use radio waves and modulation as well, but they modulate audio and video in a digital format.

The spectrum of electromagnetic frequencies available for communication is divvied up among television, radio, cellular phone systems, satellite transmission, and other communications systems. In the U.S., both the process of allocating different frequency ranges for different technologies and the allocation of frequencies within a range (radio stations, phone companies, and television stations) is under the purview of the Federal Communications Commission (FCC).

Now that we've covered some important background information, we're ready to explore the functionality of several common conventional communication and information-sharing technologies. My objective is to help you better understand how these technologies work and, at the same time, I'll highlight the strengths of the more widely used conventional technologies.

THE TELEPHONE

When you speak into your phone, the sound waves you generate pass into the mouthpiece. Here, a device that is sensitive to changes in pressure produces an electrical current, or signal. This electrical signal experiences variations in voltage that correspond directly to the changes in pressure produced by the sound waves you project. Known as output, the current then travels from your phone across a low-voltage electrical circuit into the public phone network.

In earlier analog phone systems, the electrical signal traveled through a copper cable to a central switch operated by a human being, the operator. The operator used a switchboard to physically connect the electrical circuit from your telephone to the electrical circuit of the phone you wished to call, and vice versa. If you made a long-distance call, the operator may have had to establish a connection to another switching station, or perhaps initiate a series of such connections, before the intended recipient could be connected at the appropriate remote switchboard.

Once the electrical signal generated by your telephone handset reaches the person you're calling, it is used to create variations in magnetic fields (remember that an electrical current creates a  magnetic field). These variations attract and repel a speaker cone in the phone's earpiece to recreate the original sounds you uttered at your end. The person you're speaking with drives an identical process in the reverse direction. Because of the amazing speed at which electrical signals travel, it's possible to engage in a real-time conversation over great distance.

In today's telephone system, the switching and routing of phone calls is handled by digital technology. Thus, a call is analog from your home to the local phone switch where it is converted to a digital format (described in Chapter 3). This digital information is then routed to the phone switching center that is local to the party you're calling, converted back to analog, and sent out over copper cables to the other party's phone. This final leg is known as the local loop. You'll learn more about the digital capabilities of telephone carriers and the local loop in Chapter 5, which covers digital communications technologies.

Although the phone network has grown to support digital communication among computers and other digital devices, the telephone itself is really quite limited. When you're on a phone call, all you can do is talk. You can't share documents, start a video, or transfer other information. The beauty of the telephone is its ubiquity, its ease of use, and its reliability. Almost anyone can use a phone to easily place calls around the globe.

The touch-tone handset, voice mail, call waiting, and other enhancements to the telephone have complicated its use to some degree. But the technology of the standard analog telephone basically works the same way it always has, and it continues to work extremely well, given its limitations. If you don't agree, pick up the phone, give me a call, and we can discuss it.

PRINTING

Conveying human ideas and information using pictures and words has been a core technology of civilized societies for thousands of years. Throughout time, continual technological refinements and developments have resulted in processes that churn out incredible amounts of high-quality printed material that is distributed worldwide.

Letterpress, offset, silk-screen, and gravure are among a wide variety of conventional printing processes used to print

everything from pamphlets to T-shirts. The basic idea is always the same, however. Ink is applied to paper or some other material via a process that ensures the ink only goes where it is supposed to go.

For straight black-on-white text printing on paper, the process can be fairly straightforward. The ink is applied to a surface that is either raised or recessed to match the look of the desired page. This surface may be pressed directly on paper, or it may be pressed on to an intermediary surface, which is then applied to paper.

When printing multicolored artwork or photographs, a series of photographs is taken of the original material through a screen that is offset slightly for each shot. Each screen image is used to create a grid of tiny dots that form a pattern on a printing plate. A photo is taken and a separate plate is created for each of the three secondary colors (cyan, magenta, and yellow) plus black. Each of these colors is applied in turn to recreate the artwork or photo on the page being printed. Look closely at a magazine featuring color artwork or photos, and you can see the tiny colored dots that make up the image.

Printing offers an excellent method of transmitting information, ideas, and art to audiences that are large or small, local or global. No technology is required of the recipient, and the result is portable and often lightweight. It is also a flexible medium. The size and format of the printed output, the use of color, and the overall quality can be easily tailored to specific needs.

Printing can be relatively inexpensive and extremely high-quality, but not both at the same time. It is expensive if a large audience must be reached or a very high-quality product is required, and this often limits the ability of individuals, entrepreneurs, and work groups to leverage this technology. Printing is a well-established medium that most people can relate to and use effectively, as long as they can afford the cost. While other technologies will divert some attention away from printing, it has benefits that can't be matched by any other technology. In many instances, I predict it will remain the most effective tool for disseminating information.

PHOTOGRAPHY

For over a century, photography has been a critically important medium used to capture and share images for historical, business, educational, artistic, and personal reasons. In the hands of a professional photographer, a black-and-white or color camera can create stunning images.

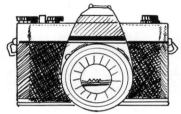

Inexpensive and easy-to-use cameras for family snapshots are readily available, and the film can be developed through any local drugstore or supermarket. You can even buy a disposable cardboard "camera in a box" for under ten dollars that will record your memories for future generations. I bought a couple of these little wonders for a trip to Wyoming with my 12-year-old son this past summer. I was delighted with the resulting photographs of mountains, prairies, streams, fish, elk, and motel swimming pools.

The core technology of the photographic process utilizes the ability of light to crystallize silver halide. In black-and-white photography, silver halide is dissolved in an emulsion that is applied to photographic film. The camera exposes the film to crystallize the silver particles. Those areas with greater exposure have greater amounts of crystallized particles, and thus appear darker. The result is a negative version of the original image on a film. In turn, this film can be projected, reversed to a positive image, and enlarged on photographic paper.

Color photography works much the same way, but color film contains three separate emulsion layers. Each layer is sensitive to one of the three primary colors (red, green, and blue). Color image processing techniques use three secondary colors as well. Cyan, magenta, or yellow dyes attach to the silver particles on the three layers in different ways to produce negative and positive images. The resulting images are used to create different types of finished products, including traditional slides and photographs.

For example, to create a color slide, each layer is dyed with the complement of the primary color for that layer. The blue layer gets a yellow dye, the green layer gets a magenta dye, and the red layer gets a cyan dye. When light is passed through the slide, each of the secondary colors absorbs light waves for one of the three primary colors, and the resulting projection recreates the original image.

The main strength of black-and-white or color photography is its ability to create high-resolution images at a relatively low cost. For professionals, the technology offers high-end equipment and high-quality results. For consumers, good quality snapshots are possible for a very low cost by using simple, easy-to-learn camera equipment. While digital photography is making some inroads, conventional photographic equipment and processes are still tough to beat.

MOTION PICTURES

A movie is a series of rapidly changing still images captured on a roll of film. When projected on a movie screen, these rapidly changing photographic images make use of the fact that a single image is retained in the human brain for a fraction of a second. For this reason, the images on the screen appear to us as a single continuous moving image that changes over time. This illusion allows movies to recreate an original scene in a two-dimensional, full-motion visual rendition. Because motion picture technology is really an extension of still photography, it offers high-quality, high-resolution moving images.

Motion picture film consists of a roll of photographic material that is perforated along its edges. It can be cut into strips and moved around during the editing process. This ability to cut and paste pieces of film is known as nonlinear editing, and it is used to create variations in the sequence of the images and the duration of scenes. Historically, film editing has also relied on laboratory chemical processes to create special effects and transitions, such as dissolves.

Early motion pictures did not include sound, but over time film engineers created a mechanism to encode audio directly onto the film along with the images. An optical track was added that could carry variations in light intensity analogous to the original sound recording. Then an optical sensor on the movie projector would convert the light intensity to an analog voltage signal sufficient to drive a sound system.

Films now include a magnetic strip to carry the audio signal, and modern movie sound systems use multiple channels of audio to create a surround sound effect. (More on magnetic sound and video recording technology later.)

Modern motion pictures also use an extra-wide screen that offers more horizontal visual real estate than other motion visual formats, such as television. Panoramic visual effects can be created that are pretty awesome when viewed in a movie theater. This wide-screen motion picture format actually came into being about the same time that television was being introduced as a new visual medium, but it was perceived as a threat to the future of the motion picture industry.

Sound and picture are recorded separately, then merged later on. Traditionally, the use of clapsticks, or a slate, at the beginning of each scene provided a visual and auditory mark that was used to synchronize the audio and video during editing. You've probably seen this before. Someone holds up the slate, reads the information on it, then claps it together to make a loud sound. Of course, modern slates are more sophisticated. An electronic marker is now used to synchronize video and audio.

Film has strength in its universality. Standard film formats are used globally, so that a film made in the U.S. can be shown on standard equipment in France, India, or Japan. This is in sharp contrast to the lack of a global standard format for television.

Most of us experience motion pictures in the theater, where their main strengths—excellent picture and sound quality—are noticeable. The motion picture industry includes segments for industrial, business, and educational films, but the use of analog video for these films is preferred. Analog video offers reasonable quality at a reasonable price and provides a quick turnaround on projects. Consequently, motion pictures outside of the theatrical entertainment realm have been all but eliminated.

Emerging high-definition television (HDTV) technology promises to deliver a motion visual and audio experience that approaches the quality of conventional wide-screen motion pictures. But I'm pretty sure we'll be going to the movies in droves for decades to come. In my opinion, you just can't replicate the big-screen movie theater experience in your own living room.

TELEVISION

Television has been around for decades. Throughout its existence, it has benefited from many technical refinements and enhancements, but the most significant has been the move to color television. The original technology developed so many years ago remains largely unchanged, and it continues to deliver interesting, informative, and entertaining video to our living rooms.

To learn more about this powerful technology, let's take a look at how your local TV station broadcasts the evening news to your living room via your antenna.

At your local television studio, the evening news is being beamed out to the local community. As the anchor sits at the news desk and speaks, a television camera is trained on her upper torso.

The camera senses the three primary colors (red, green, and blue) separately by using special light-sensitive devices, called charge-coupled devices. These devices generate an electrical signal that varies with the light energy. The camera scans thirty images per second, breaking each image into hundreds of lines. Each line contains hundreds of separate picture elements, often called pixels, and transmits them separately. The red, green, and blue pixel information, contained in a series of timed analog electrical signals, is converted to luminance (brightness) and chrominance (color) signals. The chrominance and luminance signals combine with an analog audio electrical signal that is generated by using studio microphones. The combined signal is then modulated and broadcast on electromagnetic waves via a local broadcast tower. Most stations use a VHF signal, though some stations use a UHF signal.

A television antenna on your roof is sensitive to the electromagnetic waves. It sends a low-voltage signal to your television to demodulate it, thus creating another low-voltage electrical signal that mirrors, almost exactly, the combined video signal that was modulated and broadcast at the station. Your television also amplifies the electrical signal and demodulates it into chrominance, luminance, and audio electrical signals.

If you have an old black-and-white television, it uses the luminance (brightness) signal directly to generate electron beams of varying intensity. These beams brighten monochrome video elements on the inside of your television tube. If you have a color set, it converts the chrominance signal into the appropriate mix of red, green, and blue signals. A separate electron beam for each color is used to light up red, green, and blue phosphor elements on the inside of your television screen as needed for the hundreds of pixels on each scan line. The luminance signal controls the brightness for each pixel. Your television also uses the audio signal to drive its speaker.

The television's electron beams crisscross the inside of your picture tube from left to right and top to bottom. Half the video lines are illuminated in one pass—all the odd lines in one pass, then all the even lines in the next. The beam passes from top to bottom sixty times per second, yielding an effective frame rate of thirty frames per second. This half-screen update per pass is called interlace scanning.

The human eye retains an image for a microsecond after viewing it. Like motion picture technology, television technology uses this fact to create the illusion of a continuous, moving image, so the news anchor appears to be sitting across the room from you.

One of the remarkable things about television technology is picture quality. Compared to film and computer technology, the picture resolution of television is rather poor. However, television's high frame rate and its ability to deliver a complete, unaltered, analog video signal combine to provide a picture quality most people find compelling.

There is no global standard for television video format. In North America and Japan, the format called NTSC is used. NTSC stands for National Television Systems Committee, the North American group that developed this standard. PAL (phase alternating line) is used in Europe and other parts of Asia, while SECAM (a French acronym) is used in France, Eastern Europe, Russia, and Africa.

The move to color TV technology in the 1960s was a major breakthrough as it improved the quality of the experience tremendously. Achieving chrominance and luminance in a signal that is compatible with either black-and-white or color television sets was a great feat of engineering design. Other major television technology enhancements have focused on the transmission of analog television signals to provide a much wider reach for signals and a much greater breadth of programming to choose from.

The evolution of satellite transmission is one such development. Analog television signals are modulated and carried on electromagnetic waves via satellites orbiting in space to provide global, real-time transmission of television signals. This has enabled direct satellite reception of rich programming into our homes and live global transmission of news and sporting events. The first home satellite systems used analog technology, but newer systems, such as DirecTV, use digital technology.

Satellite TV services, such as PrimeStar and DirecTV, compete with the other major television technology development, the metropolitan cable network. This technology uses fiber-optic and coaxial cable to carry television signals into your neighborhood and your home from the "head end." The head end is the cable company facility that receives signals from a variety of sources, including traditional VHF and UHF broadcasts, terrestrial microwave transmissions, and satellite transmissions. It combines these video signals, modulates them on optical and electrical signals, and then sends them out over the metropolitan cable system.

If you are on the cable system, your home can receive that signal by using a cable box or a cable-ready television. These devices demodulate and split the original signal into separate signals for dozens of channels. Then each channel signal transforms back into the original television signals containing chrominance, luminance, and audio information.

Today's television technology is an incredibly attractive medium for information and entertainment. Although television is a relatively new technology compared to many of the other conventional technologies described in this chapter, it has come to dominate much of our time and interest.

RECORDING AND EDITING AUDIO AND VIDEO ON MAGNETIC TAPE

Magnetic-tape technology allows us to capture, store, and disseminate audio and video signals easily and cheaply.

Whether news, entertainment, or documentary, the ability to combine audio and video on tape allows recording artists, editors, and engineers to create a work that is clearly greater than the sum of its parts.

To get an idea of how magnetic media recordings are made, consider the audio cassette recorder. A sound wave from a microphone, record player, or other analog sound device is received by the cassette recorder as an electronic signal. The voltage of this signal corresponds to the original varying sound wave. The electronic signal is amplified and sent over wires that are wrapped around a piece of metal. This arrangement generates a substantial magnetic field that varies as the voltage of the signal (and the original sound) varies. Then a piece of tape coated with a solution containing magnetic particles is passed over the electromagnetic field. As the signal changes, the alignment of the magnetic particles on the tape is altered.

During playback, the pattern of magnetic materials on the magnetic tape drives the variance in the fields of the electromagnet. This variance alters the electronic signal as it is transmitted to an amplifier. The amplifier recreates the original analog signal, and this signal then generates magnetic fields that cause the speaker cones to vibrate and produce the sounds you hear.

The recording process for VHS video is very similar. Because the recording process also uses an electrical signal to carry the original video, all the same principles apply. However, this is a more complex signal, carrying much more information. It includes a video signal for each pixel of video, plus audio. The tape itself moves faster, and the recording head spins as well to further increase the speed at which the signal is recorded onto the tape. Analog video signals are recorded diagonally across the tape surface, while the two sound tracks are recorded on the top and bottom of the streaming tape.

We are most familiar with the audio cassette and VHS formats, but other audio and video tape formats provide higher-quality recording. These formats are used primarily by professional audio and video producers.

Once analog video and audio are stored on magnetic tape, analog equipment can be used to combine and edit the original materials to create new recordings. This process is referred to as linear editing because the editing process generates a master tape one segment at a time in a linear fashion. Analog editing tools enable the editor to manipulate the analog signal as the master is being created. For example, treble or bass tones can be amplified in an audio recording, and brightness or contrast can be increased in a video recording.

Magnetic recording and editing technology creates a medium that allows talented artists to develop audio and video works that are appealing, informative, and entertaining. Professional productions are disseminated through well-developed channels for mass distribution.

Analog audio and video recording and editing equipment is available in different price and quality ranges to support professional and consumer applications. The technology is readily available, and consumer-grade products are well understood. This technology continues to be relied upon by many for applications in industry, business, and education as well as entertainment.

A FOUNDATION FOR DIGITAL TECHNOLOGIES

The conventional technologies we've described in this chapter form a foundation that has enabled digital technologies to evolve rapidly over the past few decades. For example:

- Phone networks now transmit digital information.
- Magnetic media, such as floppy disks, are used to record digital data.
- Electromagnetic waves are used to transmit digital information.
- Digital multimedia technologies use conventional speaker systems to create sound.
- Computer monitors use a variation of television picture-tube technology where electron beams energize red, green, and blue phosphors for each display pixel.
- Computer hardware and software now drive all sorts of printing processes, from desktop inkjet printing to high-quality camera-ready magazine layouts.
- Metropolitan cable networks are being adapted for computer-based Internet access.
- Motion pictures are being digitally altered and created from scratch with digital tools to create amazing special effects and animations.

Conventional technologies have paved the way for the digital revolution. In many instances, however, digital technologies have inherent features that provide an edge over these same conventional technologies. We'll take a close look at how digital technologies do it differently in the next chapter.

3 HOW DIGITAL DOES IT DIFFERENTLY

Digital convergence technologies offer a new paradigm for capturing, creating, manipulating, and transmitting sound, images, text, and video. The new paradigm overcomes many of the limitations of conventional communications tools, facilitating new forms of human interaction and information sharing.

When the gas-powered automobile came on the scene, some undoubtedly scratched their heads and wondered just how this new vehicle would fit in. It didn't quite have the mobility of the saddle horse, carriage, or sleigh, and it couldn't carry the passengers or the cargo of the locomotive. But it did promise to be a solid alternative that offered decent speed and a relatively comfortable ride, and it

didn't require a great deal of fuel to travel over long distances. In time, as automobile engineering and production techniques improved and the infrastructure of roads, bridges, and tunnels grew, the automobile evolved into the dominant form of transportation it is today.

Similarly, although electronic computers were invented several decades ago, it has taken time for computers and related digital technologies to evolve. Digital technologies won't entirely replace conventional communication technologies, at least not in the short term, but we now have an infrastructure and a platform for new forms of human interaction and information sharing.

New digital convergence technologies have much in common with conventional technologies. They take the same basic inputs—text, sounds, still and moving images—and produce sound and light waves as outputs. Like analog technologies, digital data is most often stored and transmitted using the properties of electrons, magnetism, and electromagnetic waves. In fact, many of the same core technologies of conventional tools have been adapted for use with digital technologies.

The digital difference lies principally in the use of a universal model for representing all forms of information. Virtually anything that can be expressed using light and sound waves can be represented as digital data.

THE DIGITAL DOMAIN

When textual, numeric, image, sound, and video information is converted to a digital format, it enters the digital domain, which is the union of digital technologies with the expanding universe of digital media. Once information enters the digital domain, the possibilities for transmitting, refining, and integrating the information with other digital media are amazing.

The desktop personal computer is one of the cornerstone technologies of the digital domain. It is an easy-to-use and standard tool for accessing, duplicating, manipulating, and storing all forms of digital media. Server computers, personal digital assistants, embedded computers, and television set-top boxes are, or will be, important components of the digital domain. But the PC is special. It's a device that millions of people can use to create globally accessible content and systems, as well as access systems and content created by others.

The personal computer, like all general-purpose computers, manipulates digital data to perform tasks or manage information. The PC uses hardware components that are controlled by software in a complex system of interactions that take place in multiple technological layers.

The lowest layer is comprised of the actual computer hardware components. At the core, a central processor unit, or CPU, electronically manipulates digital data that is represented by electronic voltages. The CPU also executes software program logic and coordinates the activity of other hardware components, such as the printer, sound card, network interface card or modem, and hard disk and floppy disk storage devices.

At the highest layer is an application software program, such as Microsoft Word or Netscape Navigator, and an operating system graphical user interface, such as Windows 98. These programs enable you to control all the electronics by clicking on the mouse and typing on the keyboard. Between the highest and lowest technological layers are other levels of necessary hardware and software that have been engineered to assure the functionality you've come to expect.

Digital communications technology is another cornerstone of the digital domain. Digital computer networks of all shapes and sizes provide fast, easy access to digital information and media, and most are now interconnected via the global Internet.

Like the personal computer, the digital communications network is also a complex set of layered technologies. At the lowest level is the physical network infrastructure, which includes wiring, digital switches, modems, and satellite receivers. At the highest level is the software used to send and receive digital data across the network. This can be an email package (Eudora), a videoconferencing system (Intel ProShare), or a Web browser (Microsoft Internet Explorer). Network engineers and software engineers deal with the layers in between to make sure that you get the data you need, when you need it, and in a format you can use.

Over the past few years, the digital domain has been extended dramatically by the explosion of the Internet. Digitized media of any type can be easily and inexpensively accessed from almost anywhere on the globe by using a standard personal computer. This is a powerful infrastructure for enhancing and extending human interaction and information sharing.

DIGITAL CODING AND CAPTURE

Whether sound, images, video, text, or numbers, the representation of all such information as discrete numeric values is the core technological concept of the digital domain. This is accomplished by converting everything to some combination of the binary digits, 1 and 0. A single binary digit is called a bit. Eight bits together is a byte, a term you will hear often.

Binary values can be represented, stored, and transmitted electronically using a variety of methods. In a computer, binary values are manipulated by transistors on tiny silicon chips. These values are stored in the computer's memory as charged and uncharged capacitors, and on computer disk and tape as differences in magnetic polarity. Binary information is also stored on a CD-ROM as pits and lands (flat surfaces) on a reflective surface. Engineers and scientists are continually exploring new methods for creating and reading binary information that may be faster, more compact, or offer greater capacity.

Different methods are used to convert the various media types into digital format. This process is referred to as digitizing, or digital capture. The digital coding schemes used to represent different forms of information vary considerably.

Text and Numbers

Text characters are represented in the digital world by unique 7-bit strings of 1s and 0s. These strings were standardized as the American Standard Code for Information Interchange and are often referred to as ASCII text, or just ASCII (pronounced ask-ee). Each ASCII character is represented in a byte. The extra bit is included for simple error checking.

character	7-bit ASCII code
A	1000001
a	1100001
B	1000010
7	0110111
8	0111000
!	0100001
$	0100100

If the text you want to use is already available in digital format, no capture is necessary. In many instances, however, you must create the text you need from scratch by using computer-based tools.

You can create and edit text on a computer with a simple text editor, such as the Notepad accessory in Windows 98, or with a word-processing or spreadsheet program. Most word-processing programs allow you to enrich raw text with special fonts, font sizes, underlining, and boldface. The resulting documents are usually referred to by mention of the tool used to create them, such as a Word document or a Pagemaker document.

Text available only in hard-copy format can be digitized in two ways. One option is to scan the hard-copy text with an electronic scanner. The scanner first captures the input document as an image and then converts the resulting image to text by using a computer program. (See the section below for more on image capture.)

This process is known as optical character recognition (OCR). The OCR program attempts to match the shapes present in the scanned image with letters and numbers. After matching each shape to a letter or number, it then assigns a corresponding ASCII value.

The OCR method offers less than 100 percent reliability, sometimes far less, depending on the quality of the original document. It is often more efficient to simply rekey the text than to go through the process of scanning and double-checking for errors.

When the original data is voluminous and in tabular format, such as the result of a survey or a lengthy table of financial figures, a data entry facility staffed with data input operators may be the best method of capturing this information. The data can be input and verified using rigorous error detection techniques, ensuring the accuracy of the result.

Humans spend a great deal of time working with decimal integers, but computers use the binary number system to store the equivalent values. The number of bits used to store a number determines the maximum value that can be represented. These binary representations are used in mathematical operations and converted to decimal values when humans need to view them. Things get a little complicated with negative values and floating-point numbers that require more complex binary representations.

In many text documents, spreadsheets, and databases, numbers are stored as plain text using ASCII codes. This is most common when the numbers are mixed with regular text and are not used in any arithmetic operations. Storing numbers as ASCII text enables alphanumeric sorting, searching, and other text-manipulation operations.

Images

Images are converted to binary format by breaking them down into a gridwork of dots. The color of each dot, or the brightness for grayscale images, is assigned a numeric value. A flatbed scanner does this by using a light-sensitive line scanner. In response to light reflected off the surface being scanned, an array of tiny photosensitive cells generates an electron flow.

The voltage generated by the cells is converted to a digital binary value. The binary values assigned are usually taken from a numeric range that is based on the use of 8 bits, 16 bits, or 24 bits. The larger numbers of bits used for coding produces a more fine-tuned and accurate color representation. Eight bits provides a range of 256 possible colors, 16 bits provides 65,536 possible colors, and 24 bits offers a range of 16.7 million color values. The number of bits used is called bit depth.

Digital cameras, which have been growing in popularity

over the past few years, work on the same principle as the flatbed scanner.

You can also use standard software, such as Microsoft PowerPoint, Word, or Excel, to create simple images, diagrams, charts, and basic graphs. More sophisticated programs, such as Adobe's Photoshop and Illustrator, let you create more complex and attractive graphics from scratch. You'll learn more about these technologies in Chapter 6.

Sound and Video

For time-based media such as sound and video, the process of converting continuous signals to a digital format is called sampling.

When sampling sound, the computer repeatedly converts an input analog voltage to a numeric value in a series of discrete time increments. The analog voltage is derived from a microphone, tape deck, or other analog source. The reverse process generates a "copy" of the original sound. If sampling occurs at a fast enough rate, this copy appears to be continuous and almost identical to the original media, because the human senses of hearing and sight will blur together the discrete sound samples.

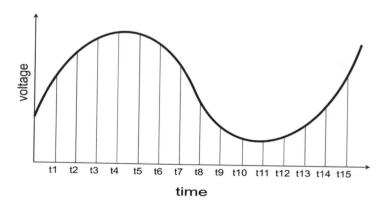

For digital video, each image is broken up by the capture process into tiny dots, just as a scanner does for image capture. These tiny dots are called pixels, which is short for picture elements. Samples occur several times per second, and each sample digitizes an entire frame of video. The need to capture a complete image in an extremely short time frame makes this process technically demanding.

As is the case with image capture, the quality of audio and video capture is dependent on the range of numeric values that are used to represent sound and light. A small number of values reduces the quality of the audio or video capture, while a larger range increases the quality. A larger range can result in tremendous increases in the amount of data generated.

The rate at which sampling occurs also has a direct impact on the perceived quality of the captured audio or video. For example, decent quality sound is usually captured using 8 or 16 bits and from 11,025 samples per second to 44,100 samples per second.

Although somewhat subjective, most people agree that quality video capture is produced using an image resolution of 640 x 480 pixels, at 30 frames per second, with 24-bit color coding. However, it is fairly common for digital convergence applications, such as Internet streaming video and desktop videoconferencing, to use video rates below 10 frames per second, with grayscale or 8-bit color video, and a reduced image size as low as 160 x 120 pixels.

At the Syracuse University School of Management, I have used a video format of 160 x 120 pixels for streaming video from our Internet video server. These videos feature distinguished speakers, such as Jack Kemp and Alan Greenspan, who have come to address our students, faculty, and members of the local business community. The most common monitor resolution setting for Windows computers is 800 x

600 pixels. On these screens, 160 x 120 pixels is the size of a book of matches, but it is sufficient for this application. It cuts down data transmission requirements, thus enabling us to provide global Internet access to some excellent lectures. The video is not high quality, but it works pretty well because we use very tight close-up shots.

Check it out for yourself at *http://www.som.syr.edu/video.*

THE DIGITAL DOMAIN—STRENGTHS AND BENEFITS

The digital domain possesses some key strengths that combine to create an extremely powerful environment.

Media Integrity

Digital media is strictly a sequence of binary values, and computers and computer networks are designed to ensure the integrity of those values whenever data is copied or transmitted. (Some important exceptions are outlined in Chapters 6 and 7.) A significant problem with conventional analog technologies is the degradation of media that occurs during reproduction. Digital technologies are able to overcome this problem.

The reproduction of original analog media introduces imperfections, commonly referred to as noise. In sound and video, this is the result of background noise and electromagnetic noise that occurs during recording. Each time the material is rerecorded, the noise increases. In an audio recording, this noise can be heard as a background hissing sound.

Similarly, any reproduction of hard-copy graphics and text generated via conventional technology is never 100 percent true to the original. Imperfections are introduced in the reproductive process, and you've surely seen this when comparing a photocopy to an original.

In contrast, digital media will not degrade when manipulated, copied, stored, or transmitted. If I email this text to you (written on an aging Macintosh Powerbook in Word 5.1 format), it will look just as good when you print it out on your laser or inkjet printer as when I print it on my old HP Deskwriter 520.

As there is no reproductive degradation in the digital realm, it is possible to digitally create a mass-produced end product, such as a popular sound recording, that surpasses the quality of the analog alternative. The superior quality of a record store CD, compared to the same recording on an audio cassette, offers a good example of this principle. The high-quality digital audio format for the Internet, known as MP3, is another good example. No matter how many times it is copied and transmitted across the Internet, MP3 retains its quality. Precisely because it is a high-quality digital format, MP3 is both attractive and threatening to the music recording industry. More information on MP3 will be provided in Chapter 7.

Media Integration

One of the most significant limitations of many conventional technologies is an inability to combine media types. For example, the telephone can only send and receive sound; printed materials are strictly limited to text and images; and while video can incorporate text, analog video formats lack the resolution required for a readable display of small text fonts.

With universal digital data and today's digital convergence technologies, it is easy to combine media because all information exists as a set of bits in the digital domain.

A prime example of the successful combination of digital media types is Web-enabled Internet streaming audio and video, where Web pages contain text, images, and embedded video streams. A second example is Internet audioconferencing and videoconferencing packages that allow users to share documents and applications.

Flexible Interactions

The unidirectional television broadcast or a one-on-one telephone conversation are examples of how conventional analog technologies are limited to only one type of interaction. Digital convergence technologies do not share these limitations. The digital domain supports a great variety of interactions that include one-on-one conferences, one-to-many broadcasts, and everything in between. In addition, these interactions can be synchronous and in real time (videoconferencing), or they can be asynchronous, such as an email discussion forum or video on demand.

Interactive Web sites, chat rooms, video and audio on demand, multiplayer Internet games, and other innovative digital communication and information-sharing tools not yet invented will offer us an unprecedented range of possible human interactions over the coming years.

Transactions

The ability to combine the transactional capability of computers and computer networks with digital media is another interactive advantage of the digital domain.

Computers have been used for decades to drive operational processes based on data input by end users. Digital convergence technologies combine this functionality with rich-media interfaces and digital networks. Aided by the Web and Internet, this capability is now fueling an explosion of Web-based consumer purchases and business-to-business commerce.

Tailoring

Software developed for digital communication and interaction is designed so that users may tailor their use of the tool and the media in a manner not possible with conventional analog technologies. For example, you can:

- set preferences in your Web browser for appearance and function;
- filter your email;
- retrieve video on demand rather than wait for it to be broadcast;
- tailor a personal Web portal with links to the information you're interested in; and
- adjust the size of the video window during a desktop PC videoconference session.

Compare this ability to tailor digital software with your television, telephone, or newspaper experiences.

Editing

Flexible and user-friendly PC-based editing tools enable both professional and lay users to create enhanced media experiences. The conventional alternatives for manipulating text, sound, images, and video are almost always more cumbersome or limited than the new digital tools.

The typewriter offers a classic example of a tool that has limited value compared to the computer's word processor. When inserting new text, moving text within the document, or deleting text, the typewriter requires you to cut and paste pieces of paper or retype the entire document to ensure a smooth flow. Of course, there is always white-out.

The digital word processor allows changes to be made on the fly. Text can be cut and pasted effortlessly, and the layout of the remainder of the document is automatically adjusted as needed.

Likewise, motion picture film editing has traditionally been a painstaking task consisting of cutting and splicing film to create the sequence of scenes that comprise the final product. Special effects required a special film laboratory. Although the nature of the medium allowed for nonlinear editing, the process itself was difficult to master.

Analog video editing is a rigid, linear process. When creating a new video, the scenes and sounds that will make up the final program are placed in the desired sequence to create a master tape. If changes to an earlier portion of a master tape are necessary, the entire master has to be recreated from the beginning. It is not possible to delete, cut, or paste video anywhere, except at the very end of the evolving master tape, without destroying the transition to, or the completeness of, the later scenes.

Digital editing overcomes these problems. Filmmakers, sound producers, and videographers are now able to manipulate their work with ease by using new digital editing tools. If the digital media is of adequate quality, the final product can be generated directly from the digital domain.

In many professional video and motion picture production environments, a hybrid digital/analog editing approach is typical. A project is first roughed out and refined as necessary by using the flexibility of the digital editor. When the principals are happy with the roughed-out version, the same digital editor generates an electronic list of cuts and transitions. This edit decision list, or cut list, is then used to create the final video or motion picture from the original high-quality analog medium.

OBSTACLES AND OPPORTUNITIES

Like anything else, digital technology has its limitations, problems, and challenges. An early awareness of two of the more pressing technical issues is critical if you are to successfully identify opportunities to deploy new digital convergence technologies.

COMPLEXITY

Complexity is one of the significant obstacles of new digital convergence technologies, primarily because these technologies rely on so many independent components that must work together flawlessly. In general, the complexity of digital convergence technology increases as you move from low-end text applications on up through higher-end applications, such as graphic images, text with images and sound, and motion video technology.

At the low end of this spectrum is text-only electronic mail. Because it is relatively simple and straightforward, most people find they can use email to send and receive text messages with little or no expert intervention. My parents finally use email. They had a tough time understanding some of the subtle features of this tool (a folder?), but they now keep in touch with a network of friends and family, experiencing only minor difficulty.

An example of complexity at the high end is desktop videoconferencing. This application uses many different technological components from numerous manufacturers that must all work together without error. You will likely need:

- a video capture card obtained from one company;
- a sound card, probably included when you bought your computer, but manufactured by another company;

♦ an ethernet card, ISDN modem, or cable modem that enables high-speed network transmission (from another vendor); and

♦ software that you use to establish and manage video sessions—from yet another source.

In addition, the technology and its configuration on your end must work with the setup on the other end.

Some videoconferencing vendors will bundle all this in a single box and support it with a single tech-support phone number, but the underlying complexity is still there. A conflict of standards, a software configuration snafu, or a quirk of one little component will too often sink your implementation efforts.

Getting desktop videoconferencing to work is something many technology-savvy users can handle, but it can be quite a challenge. Those with little or no technical background might want to think twice before launching into a videoconferencing project.

I've been exploring Internet videoconferencing solutions lately and have found it frustrating. I bought an inexpensive Logitech QuickCam Pro video camera that connects directly to a computer without the need for a dedicated capture card. Then I downloaded Microsoft NetMeeting and Netspeak's Webphone from the Internet and arranged a test with a colleague over the campus network.

My results so far have been mixed. Microsoft NetMeeting allows me to connect reliably, but the audio is poor. Webphone gives me decent audio, but the video is quirky. I have to access my video settings before I can see and send my own video. I guess this is usable for some, and even though I would love to see my parents' smiling tanned faces from Florida during the long Syracuse winters, I wouldn't recommend it to them.

Two other issues are directly linked to the complexity you often encounter. One is ease of implementation. Unfortunately, the more complex the technology and the more technologies that are involved in a given application, the more difficult and time-consuming it can be to get things up and running. The other related issue is reliability. Simply stated, the more complex a technology, the greater the chance of failure.

It's ironic that, in general, technology used to be simpler and, therefore, more reliable. It was not necessarily easier to implement, though, because earlier technologies were cruder and less accessible to nonprogrammers.

When I was a mainframe programmer in the early 1980s, most of the systems we developed were simple, straightforward, and reliable. Today, I can do much more in terms of the systems and services I can implement. My overall reach is much greater when it comes to a possible audience. But the underlying technologies have grown in complexity, and it seems I am too often explaining away bugs and glitches while mastering the art of the "workaround."

THE DATA VOLUME PROBLEM

A second major technical challenge of digital convergence technology results from the huge volume of data generated when capturing digital media. Though this isn't much of a problem for text, the data generated for high-quality digitized images, video, and sound can consume inordinate amounts of storage space. Desktop computer processors are easily overcome, and valuable network transmission capacity, or network bandwidth, is rapidly depleted.

A 4-inch x 4-inch image, captured at 300 x 300 dots per inch with a color range of 24 bits (16.7 million colors), will use 4.3 megabytes. If you sprinkle these around an electronic document, which is easy to do, you will quickly find yourself with a large document too cumbersome to work with, especially on older equipment. When transmitted to coworkers and colleagues, these large documents can easily become a drain on bandwidth-constrained digital networks such as the Internet.

4" by 4" image	4.3 MB
one minute/AM radio (good quality audio)	661.5 KB
one minute/CD (high-fidelity stereo audio)	10.6 MB
one minute/video	1.6 GB

Sound is typically captured at a rate between 11,025 samples per second and 44,100 samples per second, with each sample encoding values that use 8, 16, or 24 bits. At 11,025 samples per second and 8 bits per sample (roughly AM radio quality), one minute of audio produces 661.5 kilobytes of data, and an hour generates close to 40 megabytes of data. Using a higher-quality stereo capture of 44,100 samples per second and 16-bit samples (roughly CD quality), a minute's worth of audio generates almost 10.6 megabytes of data, and an hour produces 635 megabytes.

Digitizing sound creates large amounts of data, but digitizing video creates enormous amounts. If you digitize a standard video image of 640 x 480 pixels at 30 frames per second, with 24 bits for coding the color of each pixel, you generate an astonishing 1.6 billion bytes (gigabytes) of data per minute.

An hour's worth of video produces close to 100 gigabytes of video!

Computers processors have become very powerful, disk storage devices have dramatically increased their capacity, and networks continually achieve greater bandwidth. However, all too often these components are not up to the task when it comes to high-quality, high-end digital media. Special techniques for compressing digital images, sound, and video have been developed and implemented so that the capture, processing, and transmission of these media does not require enormous amounts of disk storage and network capacity. You'll learn more about these techniques in Chapters 6 and 7.

Digital technologies were not originally designed for the heavy-duty demands of digital media, and computers and networks are now being reengineered to more effectively handle digital convergence applications. During this transition, you must carefully consider the technical issues described here when evaluating and deploying digital convergence technologies.

Where Are the Opportunities?

If you've read this far, then the ability to accurately identify feasible opportunities to leverage new digital technologies must be important to you. As you read through this book, you will explore some of the key issues that must be taken into consideration to effectively identify and deploy digital convergence technologies. Although I've saved much of the discussion of implementation issues for the last chapter, we can get a quick preview right now. In this way, you can begin to consider some of the critical issues as you read through the coming chapters.

First, recognize that opportunities abound due to the rapid evolution of technology and the inability of many of your colleagues, coworkers, and competitors to deal with it.

There is just so much you can do, and most people lack the interest and energy to pursue these opportunities.

Take higher education as an example. All sorts of opportunities exist for applying new digital convergence technologies to enhance learning.

Most university professors have learned how to teach within a certain set of constraints. Digital convergence technologies can overcome some of these constraints, but few professors are able to carve out the time necessary to develop ideas and action plans for exploring new learning models based on this technology.

If you're a professor, there is an opportunity here for you. This opportunity might not result in a promotion or increased pay, but it could lead to exciting learning experiences for your students and some recognition for you and the job you do.

No matter what your particular situation may be, pursuing these opportunities really boils down to matching your needs and opportunities for human interaction and information sharing with the strengths of digital technology and the tools currently available. When matching needs with technologies, you must be careful to consider both the technological and nontechnical issues that will affect your successful use of these tools.

As you think through your own opportunities, an important rule-of-thumb for you to consider is that technical complexity and data volume grow as you move from text-only applications on up to video applications. Given current technological barriers, you're more likely to achieve technical success with lower-end static image- and text-based digital convergence technologies. If you are just starting out, you should consider staying within that framework. But you also may be able to gain a competitive edge if you take advantage of technologies that use more technically demanding audio and video media.

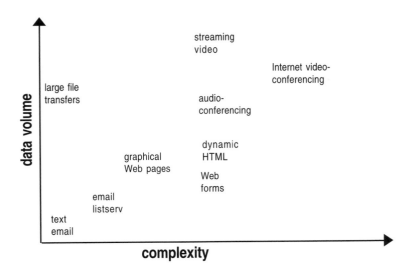

In the next three chapters, we will delve into the technological evolution of computers, computer networks, and digital media tools and techniques. Emphasis will be on the efforts currently being made to overcome the complexity and data volume constraints of digital convergence applications that were described in the previous section.

Once these problems are effectively addressed, higher-end audio and video applications will be ripe for widespread deployment.

4 COMPUTING

Personal computers now have the hardware, software, operating system capability, and network connectivity needed for many demanding digital convergence applications. The computing architecture has also evolved to stimulate and support the new digital convergence communications and information-sharing paradigm.

Since the electronic computer was invented, computers have been getting faster, smaller, and cheaper. Continual and dramatic advances in microelectronics and manufacturing processes have propelled digital computer technology forward with incredible increases in "bang for the buck," and the computing capability now available at reasonable cost is staggering by historical standards.

Over thirty years ago, Gordon Moore, one of the founders of Intel, postulated that the capacity of the microprocessor would double every year. He later revised this, predicting a doubling every two years. His predictions have become legend, and now the doubling of microprocessor performance about every eighteen months (the average of Gordon's two predictions) is known as Moore's Law. This rapid, sustained increase in computing performance has been nothing short of amazing.

The computer processor is not the only hardware

component that has benefited from dramatic technical and manufacturing advances. Computer storage devices, modems, memory modules, network interface cards, and video processors are among the other computer components that have either become much faster and cheaper or offer much greater capacity.

Most of you are probably familiar with desktop IBM PC-compatible and Macintosh computers. You should also be aware that there are other larger and more powerful  general-purpose computers that have a lot in common with PCs. They have disk drives, RAM, and network access, and they are designed for multiple simultaneous users. They also have more powerful processors, more disk space and memory, and they are more expensive. The mainframe computer is one type, and the network server is another.

In addition, there are many smaller computers, such as personal digital assistants and television set-top boxes. Computers are being embedded in automobiles, heating systems, and a variety of other devices, machines, and systems, and these computers will play an important role in our lives over the next several years.

Currently, the rapid evolution of computer technology is most noticeable as we witness the increasing power and decreasing price of the personal computer, which now delivers a potent digital experience. More importantly, the PC has emerged as a powerful tool for enabling digital convergence and empowering individuals, workgroups, and entrepreneurs. The overall architecture, including PC operating systems, software, and the back-end network servers, has evolved to provide a rich and functional computing environment.

THE EVOLVING COMPUTER ARCHITECTURE

To a computer scientist or computer engineer, "computer architecture" refers to the hardware and software that comprise a computer system. I use the same terminology to describe the way general-purpose computing devices are linked together to (1) provide functionality for end users, and (2) facilitate technology management and information management within and across organizations. A review of the evolution of computing architectures will help you understand the computing changes that are shaping the trend toward digital convergence.

MAINFRAME COMPUTING

In the '70s and '80s, mainframe computers proved their ability to manage and provide access to vast amounts of information. They enabled large organizations to automate many recordkeeping and reporting tasks. During this period, computing emerged as a major force in business and industry.

The architecture of the time featured a large centrally located computer, called a mainframe, that was shared by many users. The users were all connected via dumb terminals, usually video display tubes with a keyboard, but no onboard computing capability. Users shared the central mainframe through a mechanism called time-sharing. Time-sharing allowed each user's program to access the main processor in minuscule time slices. Once your program got a slice of processor time, it had to wait for all other users to get a time slice before getting another slice of the processor.

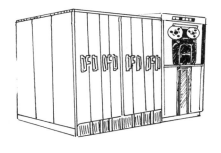

Many mainframe users lacked a terminal connection to the mainframe altogether. Instead, these users submitted hardcopy records and forms to data entry operators, who would type the information into the mainframe at terminals set up as data entry stations. The data would then be manipulated, merged, and summarized as needed. Users would receive their output in printed reports that were distributed on a daily basis. The mainframe computer processes that produced these reports were often time-consuming program runs, called batch jobs, that were executed overnight when terminal use was low.

During the mainframe era, a genre of smaller and less expensive time-sharing computers, called minicomputers, also became fairly popular. Minicomputers were deployed mostly in smaller organizations to manage information and automate clerical tasks in the same way that larger corporations used mainframe computers. Sometimes minicomputers were used in corporate departments when there was a need for local control of computing resources. For example, engineering or research and development departments needing to use specialized software might employ a minicomputer.

IBM was the dominant supplier of mainframes, and other companies, such as Amdahl, offered very limited competition. The minicomputer market was more competitive. Minicomputers were available from a number of companies that included Digital Equipment Corporation, Hewlett Packard, Data General, WANG, and Prime Computers.

THE PERSONAL COMPUTER

The PC, with its word processing, spreadsheet, and database software, took off in popularity during the '80s and '90s and spawned the creation of a whole new computing architecture.

When the desktop PC was initially deployed, it was a

stand-alone computer unable to easily share information with other PCs or with the mainframe. To transfer data from one PC to another, a user created a copy of the information on a floppy diskette and then delivered it to another user's PC. Here, the data was accessed directly from the floppy or copied to the hard drive. This technique became known as sneakernet (I suppose the data delivery was often carried out by a person wearing tennis shoes). Sneakernet was a disaster. It was inconvenient, and users ended up with multiple, and often inconsistent, versions of the same data.

Eventually, PC software was developed that enabled the PC to emulate a mainframe terminal. The PC would look and act like a terminal (as far as the mainframe was concerned), and it was connected using standard terminal wiring. Terminal emulation packages evolved to the point where users could upload and download data to and from the mainframe. This greatly enhanced the utility of mainframe data and the productivity of mainframe users.

Terminal emulation solved PC-to-mainframe information sharing, but it did nothing to address information sharing among PCs.

LAN AND WAN

The local area network (LAN) emerged in the 1980s to provide seamless PC information sharing over a network within a single location. The LAN let users share information as well as other peripheral devices, such as printers.

Some LANs enabled sharing of information and peripherals between desktop personal computers. This is called a peer-to-peer network. In a peer-to-peer network, any computer can share files and peripherals with any other computer. Appletalk (for Macintosh computers) and Artisoft's LANtastic (for PCs) were two of the most prominent peer-to-peer networks of the late '80s and early '90s.

Other LANs relied on a high-powered PC to serve as a network focal point for all network information and peripheral sharing. Known as server-based LANs, these networks allowed a personal computer to connect to a single server computer, usually at system start-up, thereby obtaining access to shared storage space, printers, and other shared services and hardware. The server computer in this architecture is often referred to as a file server. Novell Netware, a server-based LAN operating system for IBM-compatible computers, came to dominate the corporate network in the late '80s and early '90s.

The LAN was a huge success. It was also a huge first step in the shift toward an entirely network-centric computing architecture.

Initially, the LAN was confined to a small area and set of users. Within an entire corporate environment, however, it made sense to bridge the gaps so that a user on one corporate LAN could easily interact electronically with a user on another corporate LAN. Using repeaters, bridges, and routers (you'll learn about routers in Chapter 5), the LAN was interconnected and extended within a single location. But LANs at different locations were not tied together. The wide area network (WAN) solved this problem. It tied together corporate LANs that were geographically disjointed.

Remote LANs were typically linked in the WAN via connections to the telephone network. This was accomplished by using technology originally pioneered to link geographically dispersed mainframes and minicomputers.

The LAN provided a seamless network environment for

all the computing resources and users throughout a single location. Electronic mail, groupware, distributed databases, and other information-sharing technologies emerged as im-

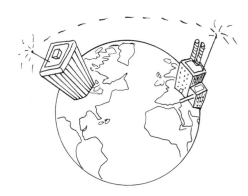

portant tools for improving productivity and communication within organizations. By establishing a WAN, these internal communication capabilities were available for even the largest global corporations. In addition, the rise

of the corporate WAN played an important role in stimulating the evolution of a global digital network infrastructure.

CLIENT/SERVER

With the advent of the LAN and WAN, together with the increasing power of the desktop PC and the network server, the role of the mainframe was called into question. If there was sufficient and relatively inexpensive processing, disk storage capacity, and connectivity in the WAN infrastructure, why not try to implement mainframe applications and services in the networked PC environment?

The mainframe was an expensive item to purchase or lease, and to maintain, and moving mainframe functions to the network promised considerable overall cost savings. Such a move would also create a more productive environment for knowledge workers because information management and access would be fully integrated with personal productivity tools on the same PC platform. The net result would be a single useful and comprehensive computing environment.

The architecture that emerged was called client/server. In this architecture, a multiuser network server provided network-connected PCs, called network clients, with access to transactional capabilities and corporate information services. Client/server was all the rage through the late 1990s.

Unfortunately, while client/server systems have a good track record when it comes to increasing productivity and overall effectiveness, these systems have often failed to deliver on the cost savings many had hoped for. The infrastructure required is more expensive and complex than anticipated. Considerable additional investments in new technology and professional technical support personnel are required to make client/server solutions work.

The deployment of new client/server systems is important in many organizations simply because these systems are Y2K compliant. Syracuse University is one organization that has had to migrate from mainframe applications to new PeopleSoft client/server technology. The University's vice president for computing has called this a "forced march." It had to be done to ensure that the University would run smoothly into the new millennium. There is even a sort of "combat pay" available for those individuals who have gone well beyond the call of duty in making the new systems work.

The transition has not been smooth, and the effort has diverted resources away from the application of technology to instruction and research. Organizations throughout all sectors of our global economy have been through a similar drill.

Client/server is an extension of the server-based LAN concept, where a shared server provides network access to corporate information systems and applications. Thin client computing is another extension that is gaining momentum in some corporate settings. Thin client computing employs a stripped-down desktop client machine that connects to a server. The server handles much of the processing burden and controls all aspects of the operating system and applications environment.

Central information technology (IT) organizations are attracted to this extreme client/server model. In addition to allowing them more management and control of the applications deployed on the desktop, it also decreases support costs and increases reliability. However, many users who have experienced the power of the PC are extremely frustrated with this inflexible bare-bones desktop client.

Although there may be situations where the thin client works well, the desktop PC is a powerful tool precisely because of its ability to empower the user. Moving to a thin client computing environment can save money, but central IT should be careful. In some cases, those cost savings won't counterbalance the opportunities lost when creative employees are stifled by such a restrictive computing environment.

INTERNET COMPUTING

Now there is a new kid on the network computing block—the Internet. During the time that LANs and WANs were being implemented by corporations, the Internet was being developed, mostly by the academic community. Internet technology has evolved to provide a complete architecture for network computing, and it has been widely adopted by government, business, industry, education, and all other organizational contexts.

The Internet uses an open method of communication that enables computers to share information regardless of their manufacturer. It replaces networks based on proprietary technology, such as Digital Equipment Corporation's DECNet, IBM's Systems Network Architecture (SNA), or Apple Computer's Appletalk. A heterogeneous mix of client and server computers from a variety of manufacturers can all be seamlessly networked together on the Internet. It also enables peer-to-peer and client/server configurations. I call this open and flexible computer architecture "Internet computing."

In the corporate environment, a private "Internet" typically disallowed outside access by use of a special computer system called a firewall. This private and internal corporate network that is built with Internet technologies is known as an intranet. A set of private network connections between or among business partners is called an extranet. These connections can be restricted by virtue of a simple password mechanism, or they may use more sophisticated technology that encrypts all data sent across the net from company to company in a secure "tunnel."

When it came to the mainframe, LAN-WAN, and client/server architectures, the consumer was left out of the loop. But Internet computing architecture is available to everyone. Any user can obtain an Internet connection via dial-up modem at a cost of $10 to $20 per month.

Internally focused corporate client/server information management and access applications can still be deployed via an intranet, but Internet computing extends beyond that. It provides a new universal accessibility that stimulates and leverages exciting developments in digital convergence technologies and applications.

There are still a few digital convergence technologies that work outside the Internet computing architecture. For example, some videoconferencing technologies bypass the Internet and use digital ISDN phone lines or other non-Internet telecommunications links. This is a temporary situation, however. High-end videoconferencing requires dedicated network connections that the Internet does not yet support. (I'll return to this topic in Chapter 5.) Internet computing is clearly the focus for those who are developing and introducing digital convergence technologies in the near and long term.

As the Internet evolves, it will gain the full network functionality required for all digital convergence applications.

WHAT'S NEXT?

Internet computing is an architecture that will eventually mature into a full-blown digital convergence architecture. This new architecture will provide connectivity not only between general-purpose computer systems— PCs, servers, and mainframes —but also between a wide variety of devices that feature embedded microprocessors and network connections. Included are television set-top boxes, scanners, video cameras, music disk recorders, personal digital assistants, portable telephones, and other devices that can be enhanced with embedded digital logic and network control. Among the latter devices are home heating systems, air conditioners, lighting systems, security systems, and who knows what else.

Java is a platform-independent software environment that will facilitate this new architecture. It includes a programming language and a Java virtual machine, which executes Java programs, that can be implemented on any type of hardware. Sun Microsystems is developing a Java-based technology, called Jini, that will make it easy to connect all sorts of devices (printers, telephones, DVD drives, video cameras, etc.) to the network.

Microsoft's Windows CE is a stripped-down Windows system for controlling and interacting with small systems and embedded computers. Microsoft has also announced its Universal plug-and-play technology that will simplify connecting a variety of devices to the network. These technologies will definitely broaden the scope of network-connected devices.

Miniaturization is another trend that has facilitated the evolution of convergence architecture. The amazing speed and capacity of the tiniest computing components now enable manufacturers to implement digital technology in almost any device you can think of. I recently heard a drive-time radio interview with a veterinarian who was touting the notion of embedding microprocessors in pets to aid in the identification of strays.

It is still too early to say whether Jini, Windows CE, Universal plug-and-play, or another technology will emerge as the pivotal technology in the move to put smart devices and embedded computers on the network. But some combination of emerging technologies will eventually create a pervasive connectivity that we are only just beginning to envision.

This digital convergence architecture will create opportunities to use computing and network technology in interesting new ways. Already I hear about a future where every machine you can think of is on the network, but I am not convinced that controlling my microwave or washing machine across the network will be all that important or useful. Being able to easily connect communication and information-sharing devices (printers, portable computers, scanners, DVD players, video cameras, and so forth) to a pervasive, ubiquitous network will be much more interesting and useful in our everyday lives. The digital convergence architecture will continue to be about connecting people and information, not appliances.

THE PERSONAL COMPUTER

At this juncture, the personal computer continues to provide the primary interface to the digital media experience for the masses. More importantly, for those of you who want to leverage new digital convergence technologies, it is the tool most often used to capture, edit, and integrate digital media and to develop digital services and resources.

The PC holds a special place as the tool that empowers individuals, entrepreneurs, and corporate workgroups. Although we will see an increasing assortment of devices connected to the network in the future, the PC will continue to be a core technology of the digital convergence architecture.

Since its introduction, the PC has seen major improvements in all its components. The result is a powerful, relatively inexpensive device ready for digital convergence applications. Sales of personal computers have risen steadily, and the PC is now a fixture on most corporate desktops and in millions of U.S. homes.

The IBM-compatible PC and the Macintosh personal computer have dominated workplace and consumer desktops for well over a decade. The Macintosh has offered strong competition for the IBM-compatible PC in the education and consumer markets, and, in the early '90s, it was beginning to make inroads in the business market as well.

When I took a position at the School of Management at Syracuse University in 1992, the administrative offices were in the process of migrating to Macs. The Mac's graphical user interface helped our staff make productive use of computer technology, and some of our faculty were exploring multimedia as well. This same scenario was also playing out at a number of U.S. business schools and in many corporations.

The introduction of the Windows 95 graphical user interface for the PC had an immediate impact. The ease of use of Windows 95, the rapid price/performance gains of the Intel chip, and the competitive forces that have driven down PC prices combined to squash any momentum the Macintosh had garnered. The Intel processor-based PC running Windows 95 or Windows 98 (dubbed the Wintel platform) has relegated the Macintosh competition to niche markets.

In the School of Management, we are just replacing our second-to-last Macintosh in an administrative office, and we have only two or three users left on Macintosh equipment among all our full-time faculty.

The Mac remains a viable computer, and the one place where it still dominates is in the publishing industry. The consultants who put together the School of Management magazine and our other promotional materials are on Macintosh. The excellent multimedia capabilities of the Macintosh also makes it the computer of choice for many digital audio, video, and graphics pros. This alone ensures that the Macintosh will stick around for some time in the new world of digital convergence, but the Wintel platform is currently gaining ground among digital media developers.

Over the past few years, one very important development has been the emergence of the low-cost PC. When an entry-level PC cost somewhere in the neighborhood of $2,000, it was a common purchase for corporations and a relatively small segment of well-heeled consumers, but it was just too expensive for the masses.

Recently, the cost of an entry-level PC has decreased dramatically, and there are now low-end PCs targeted at the consumer market priced well under $1,000. This makes the PC affordable for an increasing number of middle- and lower-income families and individuals, and the market for these inexpensive PCs has taken off.

A major factor in the price reduction of PCs is the development of the non-Intel processor. Advanced Micro Devices and Cyrix are two companies that have come out with inexpensive Intel Pentium-compatible processors. Other CPU (central processing unit) vendors are joining the low-end CPU market, and Intel has countered with its own low-end processor, the Celeron. This competition has been good for the industry, and even better for the consumer.

Let's briefly review those personal computer components (with an emphasis on the dominant Wintel platform) that ensure PC capability sufficient for many new digital convergence technologies and applications.

PROCESSOR

Clearly, the personal computer processor has benefited enormously from the performance gains predicted by Moore's Law. PC processors now operate in the range of hundreds of millions of instructions per second. CPU chips have also benefited from other refinements and developments. For example, CPUs are now equipped with very fast onboard storage (the primary cache) for data and program instructions. These performance improvements are important to digital convergence because rich-media applications place quite a burden on the processor.

In addition to the overall increases in the computing power of the PC, an important feature has been incorporated into the latest versions of the Intel Pentium processor. MMX (multimedia extensions) technology and Katmai SIMD (single instruction multiple data) are special CPU-resident instruction sets that are aimed squarely at digital convergence.

MMX and SIMD instructions are built into the chip itself, so they are very fast. These instructions are designed to accelerate the repetitive operations performed when media types, such as video, audio, animation, and images, are processed and manipulated. For example, when using an image editing program to increase the reddish appearance of an image, the same calculation must be performed on each and every pixel of data. Image editing software can be written to leverage these CPU-resident instructions, so that multiple data points can be processed in one instruction. This dramatically reduces the number of processor cycles required for this manipulation. The speedup can be significant when dealing with computer images, but video and audio operations benefit even more because the same sorts of calculations are involved over many more data points.

Media developers and designers of interactive videoconference systems for standard PCs have been constrained to low-quality video. Now, with these new CPUs, the PC can support both new uses of digital video and audio and the use of higher-quality video and audio, without requiring extra add-on processor cards.

MEMORY

Random access memory (RAM) provides data and program storage that can be accessed by the CPU at very high speeds. RAM is faster than disk storage, but it is not permanent. All information is lost when the computer shuts down, because RAM uses capacitors to store binary information as electronic voltages. These capacitors hold a charge only briefly, and they must be continually refreshed.

RAM performance and capacity has increased, and the transmission speed of data to and from the CPU has also increased. RAM has decreased in price, and it is now dirt cheap. New software routinely eats up vast amounts of RAM, and new operating systems facilitate and encourage the concurrent execution of multiple applications. This further increases the need for memory, so the decline in RAM prices couldn't have happened at a better time.

Developments in memory technology have also increased the speed and capacity of memory chips. Synchronous dynamic RAM (SDRAM) is designed to facilitate fast memory access for multimedia applications, and a new memory technology, RDRAM (rambus dynamic RAM), will take RAM performance to another level.

BUSES, PORTS, AND SERIAL INTERFACES

The CPU, memory, graphics controller, and disk controller within the computer must work together. All internal data transfer between these various components is through a high-speed data conduit called a bus. A system bus built into the motherboard (the board that includes the main system components) enables high-speed communication between the CPU and main memory. Communication between the system bus and the other components of the computer is through a bridge connector in the motherboard to another high-speed bus, called an expansion bus.

Communication between external devices and the expansion and system buses of a PC occurs in two ways. Special connectors on circuit boards, or cards, are installed in computer expansion slots that connect directly to an expansion bus (for example, a network card); or a serial interface, or port, on the edge of the motherboard is accessed through a hole in the side of the system (for example, a serial port that accepts your external-modem cable).

PCI Bus and AGP Port

As computing evolved, the expansion bus of the standard PC, called the ISA (industry standard architecture) bus, became a bottleneck. A new bus was developed a few years ago to provide greater capacity for internal data transfer. This bus, the PCI (peripheral component interface) bus, offers an internal data transfer rate of up to 128 million bytes per second. The PCI bus has a theoretical maximum of four times that transmission capacity, but it may be some time before standard desktop PCs are equipped with such a bus. Silicon Graphics, however, has created a high-end Intel-based graphics workstation that touts very high PCI throughput.

The PCI bus has been used to handle video traffic, but

even at 128 million bytes per second, a bottleneck can occur when 3D graphics or full-motion video is being delivered. The advanced graphics port (AGP) is a new high-speed bus dedicated to handling video traffic. This technology is aimed directly at the anticipated growth of motion and 3D video media as digital convergence takes off.

USB and Firewire

In the past, expanding the capabilities of the PC meant connecting a device to a low-speed serial or parallel port, or installing an ISA or PCI circuit card. This was a problem. Installing ISA and PCI cards is a pain in the neck, and parallel and serial ports are just too slow for today's rich-media digital convergence applications. Universal serial bus (USB) and firewire are two new high-performance options for expanding the PC.

USB is based on a technology standard crafted by a consortium of hardware, software, and peripherals manufacturers. USB can connect multiple external devices in a daisy-chain arrangement at a speed of 12 million bits per second. Most new PCs are now shipping with a USB port. Printers, video cameras, and speaker systems are among the devices that can be connected to a USB port.

The Institute of Electrical and Electronics Engineers (IEEE), a professional engineering society, has standardized an alternative serial bus called firewire. Officially known as IEEE 1394, firewire is much faster than USB, boasting speeds of up to 400 million bits per second. This transfer rate can even support demanding digital video applications. As of this writing, very few computers are shipping with firewire, but that will surely change over the next few years. Other devices, such as television set-top boxes, will also be shipped with firewire interfaces. Firewire is so fast that the emergence of a firewire device bay is predicted. This bay will be used to attach devices, such as disk drives, that are now permanently mounted in the PC enclosure.

VIDEO AND SOUND

Continual and rapid advances in computer display technology constitute another significant aspect of PC evolution that stimulates and supports digital convergence applications and technologies. Computers use special hardware for processing and outputting a video signal to a CRT monitor. These hardware components have also benefited from the price/performance gains in chip technology and memory. Today's video processor is very fast, and it has several megabytes of onboard memory. This is sufficient for a highly detailed video display using millions of colors at resolutions of 640 x 480 pixels, 800 x 600 pixels, 1024 x 768 pixels, and higher.

Computer monitors have evolved to accommodate these high-resolution displays that go far beyond the line resolution of your television set. The computer monitor does an excellent job of displaying small graphics and text, which would be unreadable on a conventional television set. New flat monitors based on liquid crystal display (LCD) technology offer a slimmer, brighter image that is really quite stunning. Right now, these panels are still expensive, but you can expect prices to drop dramatically over the next couple of years.

Although you have excellent video resolution on your computer monitor, digital video often looks mediocre, even crummy, when compared to the very attractive video on the living room television set. The problem is not the resolution of your monitor and video system. Rather, the poor-quality video results from the inability of your processor or network to transmit the enormous volume of data required for high-quality digital video. As a result, many people don't realize that the resolution of the computer display is actually of better quality than that of the TV.

If you doubt this, get up close and personal with your TV and your computer monitor. When you actually see the individual pixels that make up the picture on each screen, it will become clear that the computer monitor has a superior resolution.

The inclusion of a high-quality sound card as standard equipment on desktop computers is another significant development that stimulates and supports digital convergence. The 16-bit stereo card has become a standard, offering high-fidelity stereo sound. Unfortunately, the speakers that ship with many new computers usually leave something to be desired. The same card can be used to drive a speaker system or capture digital audio in stereo CD-quality format. Many digital convergence applications already leverage sound as an integral aspect of the user interaction.

PC sound is undergoing changes that will further the fidelity and quality of the sound you hear. One development is technology that enables 3-D sound. This will be useful for entertainment and for business applications, such as videoconferencing. Another development will separate the analog portion of the sound system from the computer enclosure. Because the computer enclosure has a great deal of electromagnetic noise, this will ensure a cleaner and clearer analog sound signal to the speaker system.

NETWORK ACCESS

The network interface card is another critical PC component that makes the corporate PC a viable user interface for digital convergence applications. The ethernet network has become a corporate standard, and a PC ethernet card can accommodate a data transmission rate of 10 million bits per second. New ethernet cards that can handle a whopping 100 million bits per second and more are beginning to replace the standard ethernet card. (You'll find a more detailed discussion in the next chapter.)

Cable modems, satellite transmission, and other technologies can provide consumers with high-speed Internet access options, but most consumers still use a modem to connect to the Internet over standard analog telephone lines. Modem speeds continue to increase, and the latest modems can operate at a theoretical top speed of 56K bits per second. Normally, however, only two-thirds of that theoretical maximum is achieved. This is entirely adequate for reasonable audio transmission, but it is sufficient for only very low-quality network video.

Disk Storage

Hard disk storage is another rapidly evolving PC component that enables digital convergence. Today's PC hard disks now have a capacity range of tens-of-gigabytes, and the transfer rate from disk to processor for high-performance disk drives is in the range of tens-of-megabytes per second.

High-capacity disks are a boon for anyone developing digital media. The volume of data required to digitally represent images, audio, and video is a constant drain on disk storage resources. Today's hard drives are a huge help to the media developer when storing, retrieving, and managing digital media during capture and editing.

While the PC's internal hard disk has grown in capacity and increased in speed, so too has removable storage media, another storage medium important to digital media developers. It is very expensive to acquire enough storage capacity on hard disk for complex digital media projects that use many images or lots of audio and video. Today's digital media developers can turn to removable media as a very effective, low-cost storage medium. Not only does it expand available storage, it also provides a convenient portable format for transferring large amounts of data between machines.

For example, the popular Zip drive holds 100 megabytes in a compact disk that can be inserted and removed, much like a regular floppy drive. A Zip drive costs around $50 and each disk costs under $10. The Zip Plus drive, costing a couple of hundred dollars, can hold 250 megabytes. Other removable storage technologies offer much higher capacity, such as the Jaz drive with a capacity of one gigabyte. Faster, larger removable storage options are more expensive, but still quite reasonable.

OPERATING SYSTEMS

A computer operating system is the software that manages the computer's hardware components. It is a set of programming interfaces that allows the developers of software applications to implement various computer functions. As an interface for the user, it starts programs, copies files, configures hardware, and installs software.

Most consumer-owned personal computers run the Macintosh MacOS operating system or Microsoft's Windows 95 or 98 operating systems. Many corporate desktop computers use a higher-performance operating system from Microsoft, called Windows NT, that is both more reliable and more secure.

Today's PC operating systems include some important

technical improvements. They offer application programming interfaces (APIs), such as DirectDraw and Direct3D, that software designers can use to exploit the increased capacity and functionality of new hardware technologies. Modern PC operating systems are also designed to overcome some of the memory and hard-disk limitations of earlier operating systems, as well as facilitate and encourage the concurrent execution of multiple programs.

Current operating systems offer a friendly graphical user interface, or GUI (pronounced gooey). The Macintosh has always had a GUI, and it has always been fairly easy to use, giving the Mac an advantage for many years. Earlier PC operating systems, such as MS DOS and versions of Windows prior to Windows 95, employed GUI interfaces that were cumbersome and unreliable, or lacked GUI interfaces altogether. With the introduction of the Windows 95 and Windows NT GUI operating system interfaces, the PC took a dramatic step forward, and the Macintosh no longer has a clear-cut ease-of-use advantage.

One of the great things about a GUI operating system interface is that much of what you learn about your first application software is transferable to other software you may want to use. When a user fires up a new application, there will be lots to learn, but many of the basics will be old hat. Tasks such as how to save or print a file, or how to select, edit, and move text, will be the same. This simple fact has turned out to be quite powerful.

Another ease-of-use feature that the Macintosh has had for some years is now available in Windows 95 and Windows 98. Called plug-and-play, this feature enables the operating system to recognize and automatically configure many third-party hardware components. When plug-and-play works, it is very easy for users to add new hardware and peripherals, thereby increasing the performance or capacity of their systems.

Contrast this with the DOS and Windows 3.1 era, when new hardware required an installation procedure that tested the technical skill and patience of the installer. Unfortunately, plug-and-play doesn't work all the time. A user who installs a modem, sound card, or disk drive is still sometimes forced to deal with tricky and time-consuming configuration.

The renewed emphasis on ease of use when designing today's PC operating system enlarges the audience for computing technology beyond the nerds and geeks, thus including a much greater percentage of the general population.

A WORD ABOUT NOTEBOOKS

Many engineering advances have focused on miniaturization, and one result is a small portable version of the desktop computer called a notebook, or laptop computer. These computers typically weigh from four to eight pounds, have a compact keyboard, and a trackpoint, scratch pad, or trackball instead of a mouse. The display is flat and compact, but it is often more difficult on the eyes than a standard monitor. Notebook computers come with standard hardware, including Intel processors and large, fast hard drives.

Some computer components were developed specifically for the notebook.

■The notebook display uses active matrix and LCD technology that is different than that of a standard CRT monitor.

■Notebook "docking stations" and "port replicators" let you use a notebook with a regular keyboard, mouse, monitor, and other desktop PC components.

■Notebook computers have PCMCIA card slots. (Don't worry about the acronym; no one can remember it!) These are small thin slots in the side of a notebook computer that allow you to easily plug in and configure a variety of devices, such as modems, ethernet cards, and CD-ROM drives.

The notebook computer is somewhat pricey compared to the desktop personal computer, but it has proven itself as a capable, durable, and easy-to-use device. It provides a solid platform for digital convergence technologies and applications for users who are on the go.

I recently attended a training session on streaming video technology. The presenters used notebook computers for everything. The notebooks did audio and video capture, editing, and encoding; they were configured as Web servers and video servers; and, of course, notebooks were used for all the presentations and demos. The presenters commented that it was very easy to pull off such training sessions using only a few notebook computers. The processing power and storage capacity of today's compact and lightweight notebook computer is truly amazing.

SERVERS

Although the desktop computer is a critical platform for many digital convergence technologies and applications, there is another important side to the digital convergence equation—the network application server. Some applications use desktop-to-desktop computer interaction (for example, desktop videoconferencing), but many applications require a dedicated server that can deliver shared services and resources to many users.

A Web server is a good example. When you start up a Web browser on your PC and enter a Web address to connect to a specific Web site, you are actually connecting to a server machine that is shared by anyone else who wants to access that Web site.

There are many other examples of application servers that play a critical role in digital convergence applications.

■Multipoint videoconference servers enable multiple remote videoconference users to interact in one conference.

■Email servers act as electronic post offices, enabling the transmission and receipt of email by individuals and groups.

■Database servers provide users with easy access to large stores of information.

■Media servers deliver real-time and on-demand access to audio and video.

Server computers range from regular desktop computers equipped with server software (for those applications where only a few users access the server on an infrequent basis) to high-end multiprocessor servers that can handle many simultaneous users.

Many application servers use the same technology that

is found in the desktop computer, including an Intel processor, standard memory modules, and a standard disk drive. For increased performance and reliability, Wintel servers are often equipped with high-end hardware components, such as high-speed and high-capacity hard disks, tape backup units, and lots of RAM. They sometimes have multiple Intel processors, and they typically use the Windows NT operating system rather than Windows 95 or Windows 98. They are also much more expensive.

Other servers use one or more high-performance RISC (reduced instruction set computer) processors. These are high-end servers that are purchased from manufacturers such as Hewlett Packard, Sun Microsystems, and IBM. They use an operating system, called Unix, which has been under development within corporate and academic environments for decades. RISC-based Unix servers are usually the servers of choice for the more taxing digital convergence applications. For example, the most frequently accessed Web sites and the most heavily used video servers run on RISC-based Unix servers.

A recent variation on these two themes is the use of a noncommercial public domain version of Unix on an Intel-based server. Called Linux, this option offers the elegance of the Unix server on increasingly powerful PC equipment, and thus provides a very capable server at a very reasonable cost.

For some time, the lack of commercial support for Linux was seen as a negative, but the Linux open software model has proven quite effective. A solid community of programmers exists who have ensured the quality of Linux. More and more, system administrators now see Linux as a superior Unix operating system.

Developments in processor speed, memory, disk storage, and operating system technology have driven the evolution of the desktop computer and have also positively impacted server technology. Today, servers are capable of supporting many demanding client/server-style digital convergence applications.

Now let's turn our attention to the most important and, in some ways, most intriguing underlying component of digital convergence—the network.

5 DIGITAL COMMUNICATIONS TECHNOLOGY

Digital networking is the linchpin of digital convergence. It is also the delicate mechanism that too often falters, disappointing our efforts to leverage the technologies of this infant phenomenon. This chapter explores the characteristics and the trends of digital communications technologies to help attune you to the promise and realities of this critical aspect of digital convergence.

Digital communications technology has evolved mainly within the context of two converging venues. The first, the voice-only telephone network, was once an end-to-end analog network. It is now largely a digital network, and its evolution has seen the development of high-capacity long-haul digital links. The second venue, digital computer networks, has emerged over the past couple of decades to enable seamless data sharing among interconnected computers.

The current result of the rapid evolution and convergence of digital technology in these two venues is a high-speed digital network infrastructure capable of transmitting voice, video, and data. Many broadcast technologies originally developed as analog, such as satellite technology and cable television technology, are being adapted to transmit digital signals. These ongoing adaptations further extend the ubiquity and the utility of this global digital network infrastructure. The

Internet is a global and public incarnation of this phenomenon that is poised to become *the* network of our planet.

Our rapidly evolving network infrastructure removes geographic barriers, providing immediate anytime, anywhere access to electronic resources and electronically connected humans. This is the single most powerful element underlying digital convergence, but it is also the most tenuous. Although the Internet is the foundation network and starting point for this revolution in technology, we need to understand that it is an adolescent infrastructure that lacks reliability, robustness, and security. The degree to which digital convergence impacts our lives and our businesses will be driven by the evolution of digital communications technology, in general—and the Internet, in particular.

TYPES OF NETWORKS

To better understand how networks are evolving in the age of digital convergence, let's briefly compare and contrast digital computer networks with the conventional network technologies that have enabled communication for many decades.

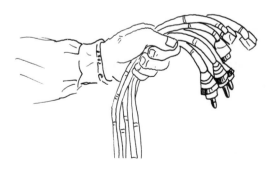

VOICE

Telephone networks were built around the notion of a single circuit established for the duration of a one-to-one voice conversation. Recall the discussion in Chapter 2 of the switchboard operator who would connect you and the person you're calling. In the beginning, the circuit was an analog electrical connection dedicated for the length of the call.

In modern phone networks, the analog portion of your call ends at a local phone company switch. Here, the call is converted to digital format and routed in a data stream across the local and long-distance carrier digital networks, passing through local and remote digital switches as needed. When the call reaches the phone switch that is local to the party you're calling, it is converted to an analog signal for the receiving phone.

While a call is in the digital portion of the network, it is combined with other phone calls and routed between switches in a single digital transmission. The total digital data transmission capacity (known as bandwidth) of the digital pipeline is divvied up among all the separate voice calls sharing that bandwidth. This is done via time-division multiplexing, which is a time-based algorithm that gives each call a slice of the available bandwidth. Time-division multiplexing is similar to the mainframe time-sharing mechanism discussed in Chapter 4.

The digital voice network is a "circuit-switched" network. It dedicates network bandwidth for each digital phone circuit, and this allocation guarantees a clear, reliable call. Network engineers call this QoS, or quality of service. QoS is a characteristic that most of today's digital computer networks lack.

Voice traffic is digitized and then transmitted in circuits that ensure a continuous, sustained data rate of 64 Kbps (kilobits per second), and the long-haul transmission lines that carry time-division multiplexed phone calls are configured in multiples of 64 Kbps. A T1 line has an aggregate bandwidth of roughly 1.5 Mbps (megabits per second) and can handle twenty-four simultaneous voice circuits (1.5 Mbps divided by 64 Kbps equals 24). A T3 line is a 45 Mbps pipe that can handle 672 circuits. High-capacity long-haul networks, such as the synchronous optical network (SONET), use fiber optics and can handle many more circuits. A SONET OC-3 network has 155 Mbps of bandwidth, handling over 2,000 circuits, and an OC-12 has a capacity of 622 Mbps, enough to handle just over 8,000 voice circuits.

BROADCAST

Analog broadcast networks—including FM and AM radio, and UHF, VHF, and cable television systems—transmit analog signals in electromagnetic waves, or voltage signals. (These transmission modes are described in Chapter 3.) They offer high-quality audio and video media delivery to a large number of users using modest bandwidth. Broadcast networks aren't stressed because they are limited to a one-to-many unidirectional flow of information over a finite signal range.

Broadcast networks are noninteractive, employing a delivery model of continuous scheduled content. To receive specific content (a program), you must know the schedule and then tune in when the programs you want to see or hear are broadcast. We've all come to live with this, and we accept it without thought, but it is a constraint on our access to audio/video media that can and should be overcome.

Digital transmission is increasingly used for broadcasts. It appears as HDTV broadcasts over the local airwaves in major television markets, as satellite broadcast networks (DirecTV), and as a new cable television option in some cities.

COMPUTER

Computer networks move information across the network in small chunks of data, called packets. For example, when you send an email message to a friend or colleague, your message is broken down into packets, each tagged with an address and then sent out on the digital network. These packets are routed through the network via "best effort" delivery, meaning they get to their destination in no particular order and with no special priority or guaranteed rate of transmission. When the packets are received by the hardware and software of the destination computer, they are reassembled into the original message.

This packetization and transmission model applies to any type of digital data that is transmitted, whether an email message, a video stream, or an Excel spreadsheet. In contrast to the circuit-switching mechanism of the voice network, computer network data transmission uses "packet switching."

Digital computer networking is based on the concept of an open and shared transmission medium. Packets may be routed on different paths to reach a particular destination computer. Sometimes packets are lost and must be retransmitted. Also, there is no prioritization. Email traffic has the same priority as interactive video, and all transmissions will occur only as fast as the network will allow.

Computer networks use available bandwidth more efficiently than the voice network, which dedicates 64 Kbps for the duration of each call, even if no one is talking. In a computer network, unused bandwidth is fully available for any application that needs it. This works well for many types of computer data.

Web access and database transactions are much different

than voice calls. These are quick hits where a relatively small amount of data is transmitted. The shared network delivers this data as quickly as possible in a burst transmission.

Although packet networks make efficient use of network bandwidth, there is a downside. When too many devices are trying to transmit a lot of data as fast as possible, the contention for available bandwidth results in congestion.

Voice and video have complicated the picture. Time-sensitive data, such as voice and video, require a continuous and reliable transmission. For one-way streaming audio and video, an uninterrupted, continuous stream is actually more important than delivering the data as quickly as possible. For interactive video and audio, minimal delay is also important. A delay of more than a couple of hundred milliseconds in an interactive voice conversation or videoconference is noticeable and can disrupt the cadence of the conversation.

When network congestion occurs, it disrupts the steady flow of real-time media. Overtaxed routers (described later in this chapter) often introduce some delay, or latency. When severely overloaded, they actually discard packets. Also, when high-orbiting geostationary satellites are involved in the transmission, there is a noticeable delay due to the distance the signal must travel.

If you've ever heard garbled audio or seen freeze-frame video on the Internet, you know that the open "send it as fast as you can" packet-switched Internet isn't yet ready to replace voice and broadcast network technology. But digital packet-switched networks will challenge, and may eventually replace, these conventional networks for the following reasons:

■ Like the voice network, the digital computer network is designed for reliable communication between any two points (computers). Although packet-switched computer networks lack the quality of service we receive from the phone network, the networking and telecommunications industry is feverishly working to implement QoS for packet-switched networks, including the Internet.

■Even though computer networks are not broadcast networks, client/server systems offer one-to-many interaction. In many physical networks, such as an ethernet LAN, it is possible to broadcast information to all client machines. Also, a pseudo-broadcast mode is now being deployed throughout corporate networks and the Internet. Called multicasting, it can broadcast to all computers subscribed to a particular Internet or intranet media stream. Multicasting will be described in more detail in Chapter 7.

As the momentum builds for full-blown digital convergence, the end-to-end digital network is emerging as the network of choice for all forms of communication. Consequently, we are seeing incredible investment in network research and development.

DIGITAL COMPUTER NETWORK LAYERS

As you recall from Chapter 3, digital networks are comprised of a series of technological layers. A standard layered network model was developed by the International Standards Organization as the OSI (Open Systems Interconnection) network. This model defined seven network layers. Although no real network, not even the Internet, has implemented all seven layers, the OSI model has been a useful tool for explaining and understanding how various network components work together.

To make network layering even easier to understand, I'll boil it down to three distinct sets of layers.

The lowest set of layers is that of the physical data network. These layers include physical wiring, connectors, PC circuit cards that connect to the network (a network interface card, or NIC), electronic devices that can facilitate or manage network traffic, and protocols that dictate physical network data format and transmission.

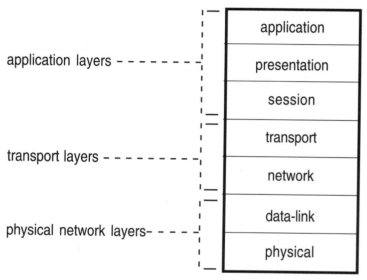

In the next layers, we get into a more abstract set of communication standards that define the configuration of data packets, packet addressing, and transmission. These are the network transport layers that enable digital communication throughout interconnected networks.

The third set of layers, the network application layers, provides high-level application protocols and standard programming interfaces for applications programmers.

Because these layers are technologically isolated, they can evolve independently. They can also be upgraded independently within an organization.

For example:

■Networking providers can invent and adapt new hardware technologies that offer improved performance without concern for the applications interface.

■An organization's physical network infrastructure can be upgraded to enable bandwidth-hungry multimedia applications, without disrupting existing applications.

■Network engineers can develop application protocol standards to support the new demands of real-time multimedia data transmission. These new or improved protocols can then be deployed over any existing physical network infrastructure.

■Applications developers can create new software that utilizes the network, without concern for the physical network that the software will run on.

■You can upgrade the modem in your home from a 28.8 Kbps modem to a high-speed cable modem without reinstalling your Internet application programs. Your browser will continue to work the way it always has once you've completed the upgrade, only faster.

A quick review of the three network layers described above will help you to understand the capability of the evolving network infrastructure.

PHYSICAL NETWORK LAYERS

The physical network layers include wiring as well as the computer and peripheral equipment interfaces that physically connect the network. These are also the layers at which the electronic, electromagnetic, or optical signaling systems carrying digital 1s and 0s are defined and implemented. Organizing the bits carried by the lower-level electronic or optical signaling system into some useful aggregate data structure is the job of hardware layer protocols, such as ethernet.

For ethernet, the aggregate data structure is called a frame. It resembles a packet, except it exists only within an ethernet network. Similar protocols exist for digital packet transmission over a wide variety of physical networks, from low-speed modem connections over analog phone lines to high-performance fiber-optic SONET networks.

The LAN

The physical computer networks most people first came in contact with were local area networks. LANs allowed PCs and PC servers to communicate for the purpose of sharing files and peripheral devices, such as printers. The first widely deployed PC LANs used a coaxial cable to transmit data. This is the same thick cable containing a single thin wire that is used for cable television. Individual PCs hooked up directly to the coaxial cable via another special cable and a connector, called a tap.

Ethernet emerged as the dominant LAN protocol, although IBM's token-ring LAN technology was a competitive alternative at one time and is still used in some settings. Early Apple Macintosh networks used inexpensive phone cabling for LAN networking that operated at very slow speeds. Eventually, Macintosh networking was adapted to run over ethernet as well.

The typical early ethernet LAN used a bus topology. The devices on the LAN shared a single data conduit, called a bus, which was the coaxial cable. The coaxial cable bus evolved to a new hardware infrastructure called a hub. In this system, the bus was collapsed into a single box, and a series of long and inexpensive twisted-pair copper cables connected the hub to each of the computers on the network.

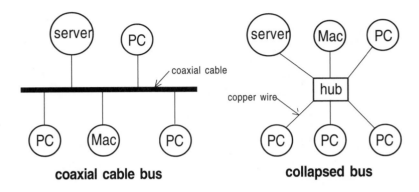

coaxial cable bus　　　　　　　**collapsed bus**

Like the coaxial cable of the early LAN, an ethernet hub is a collapsed bus shared by everyone on the LAN. A coaxial cable-based ethernet bus, or an ethernet hub, is referred to as shared media.

Original ethernet networks ran at a maximum capacity of 10 million bits per second. The base speed of ethernet has increased, and an ethernet speed of 100 Mbps is now being widely implemented in networking gear. A more recent ethernet standard allows networks to run at a whopping billion bits per second!

In today's typical 10 Mbps or 100 Mbps shared-media ethernet network, each device on the network has a unique address electronically stamped on its ethernet card. Ethernet protocols ensure that computers accept only those frames sent to them. The hub is the bus, and the total aggregate transmission capacity of the LAN is contained within the shared hub. As a result, you and your PC achieve a transmission speed of 10 Mbps or 100 Mbps only when most of the other PCs and servers on the network are idle. Obviously, this will not happen very often.

Over the past few years, the shared hub has evolved into something called a switch. This device is similar to the hub, but it has a very high-speed backplane data conduit. Computers

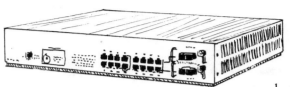

are connected to the switch via twisted-pair copper wiring, and packets are switched directly from one device to another at a guaranteed rate of 10 Mbps or 100 Mbps (depending on whether the switch supports standard ethernet or the newer, faster 100 Mbps ethernet). Ethernet running over twisted-pair wiring, with shared hubs or switches, is now the standard for corporate LANs.

Interconnected LANs

The isolated workgroup ethernet LAN is only part of the physical network. In large organizations, LANs are interconnected to create an enterprise network.

A router is an intelligent device that sits between networks. It examines the packets on each of the networks it is connected to, identifies those packets destined for another network, and routes them to the appropriate network as needed. The router is a special-purpose hardware device that connects physical networks, so it is included here in the description of the physical network layers. But it also services the network transport layers. The router understands transport layer network protocols and, therefore, determines whether a packet gets routed to one of the connected networks.

Early routers were just general-purpose computers programmed to perform this function. Each packet had to be routed by a routing program that ran in the computer's memory. As traffic increased, routers too often couldn't keep up, dropping packets and creating bottlenecks. This still happens all too frequently on the Internet.

To speed up things up, router vendors have added hardware circuitry that performs some of the functions of routing at "wire speeds." They do this with application-specific integrated circuit (ASIC) technology.

In recent years, switches have also been used to interconnect LANs. When switches were first used in this role, they provided a lower-level connectivity that didn't utilize transport layer packet information. Now, transport layer routing functions have been added to network switches by using ASIC technology. The new switches have routing functionality built in and are used to interconnect networks.

WAN

A wide area network (WAN) links geographically remote networks together. Typically, the long-haul network infrastructure of a communications carrier, such as Bell Atlantic, AT&T, or Qwest, is accessed by a router at each end of every WAN connection. WANs interconnect a mix of physical networks. They utilize copper cable, fiber-optic cable, satellite, and microwave connections. WAN connections for large enterprise networks usually run over leased T1 lines at 1.5 million bits per second, T3 connections at 45 million bits per second, or fiber-optic links that can run from tens of megabits per second to gigabits per second.

Fiber-optic cabling dominates the backbone segments of our major telecommunications carriers. For over a decade, fiber-optic long-haul networks have used the same time-division multiplexing that is common with copper-based T1 and T3 lines. It is not unusual to see SONET backbone networks running at OC-48 speeds (2.5 Gbps), and we should see an OC-192 backbone at 9.9 Gbps by the time you read this.

A new approach for transmitting data over optical

media, known as dense wave-division multiplexing, is being developed and deployed. This technology splits the light spectrum in a fiber cable into many high-speed channels, dramatically increasing available bandwidth. The future of network backbone bandwidth based on fiber-optic technology looks very bright, indeed.

ATM

Asynchronous transfer mode (ATM) is the network technology most often used in backbone fiber-optic networks. Network transport protocols, such as the Internet protocols described below, run over the top of the ATM connection. Therefore, we include a description of ATM in the physical networks section, even though it is actually much more than that.

ATM was developed as a solution for all portions of the digital network infrastructure. It was designed with a hybrid packet-switching/circuit-switching scheme and QoS. Tiny packets, or cells, consisting of 48 bytes of data plus 5 bytes for control information, are transmitted across an ATM network through a series of network switches. ATM works across all the network layers and includes hardware-level network protocols, network transport protocols, and application interfaces.

ATM is significantly different than ethernet, and replacing ethernet with ATM in the LAN is costly. As higher-speed ethernet options become available—such as switched ethernet, 100 Mbps ethernet, and gigabit ethernet—there is even less reason to rip ethernet technology out of the enterprise and replace it with ATM.

However, ATM has caught on in the long-haul WAN telecommunications infrastructure. Most national telecommunications carriers and Internet service providers are implementing ATM in their backbone networks for private corporate WAN connections and for the Internet backbone infrastructure. ATM can run over fiber-optic cables at hundreds of megabits and gigabits per second, and its bandwidth management can be used to create virtual circuits that offer different QoS performance levels.

The 5 bytes of control information included in every 53-byte cell eat away at the underlying bandwidth. Also, because ATM cells are very small, a great deal of processing is required to both break up larger packets entering the ATM network and then reassemble them when exiting. Network engineers refer to these ATM realities as the ATM cell tax. An emerging option will run Internet transport protocols directly over an underlying fiber-optic network connection, thereby cutting ATM out of the picture altogether and eliminating the ATM cell tax.

Remote Internet Access

Consumer access to the Internet occurs most often through a local wired connection. This connection is known as the local loop or the last mile.

For those who dial up to the Internet, incoming and outgoing data is modulated and demodulated over an analog phone line via a modem. Increasing the speed of modems from 28.8 or 33 Kbps to 56 Kbps helps consumers and other users in the local loop, but it is just not enough. The average 56 Kbps modem connec-

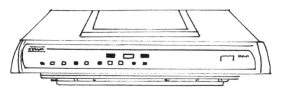

tion actually yields a little more than a modest 30 Kbps. Using a 56 Kbps modem, you get a dribble of data instead of a drip.

ISDN, the fully digital phone line option now widely

available, offers a transmission rate of 128 Kbps. This is a significant increase over modem speeds. Unfortunately, configuring and troubleshooting ISDN is still rather complex, so it is not a good option for the average nontechnical consumer.

Fortunately, new high-speed options are becoming available from cable television providers, telephone companies, and satellite services. We'll discuss these technologies fully in the section titled "Obstacles."

NETWORK TRANSPORT LAYERS

Network transport protocols are technical specifications that define the rules and procedures governing the formation, transmission, routing, and receipt of packets. The first network transport protocols were proprietary protocols designed for the homogenous networks of a specific type of computer, such as Novell Netware or Appletalk.

These proprietary protocols were effective in a tightly controlled network environment, but they came up short as the need to accommodate a wider variety of computers and physical network components grew. Proprietary protocols are still widely used and are required for some LAN services and applications.

Internet protocols were designed from the ground up to support a heterogeneous network environment that can include a wide variety of physical networks. These networks include ethernet, microwave and fiber-optic links, telephone modem connections, and digital satellite downlinks. An Internet network (that is, any network that uses the Internet protocols) can also service a plethora of computing devices, from palm computers to the most powerful mainframes. Whether running on the public Internet or private corporate networks, the Internet protocols have become the dominant network transport protocols for all computer networks in the last five years.

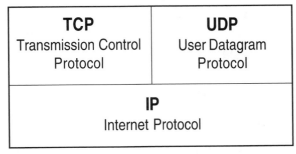

TCP Transmission Control Protocol	**UDP** User Datagram Protocol
IP Internet Protocol	

Internet network transport protocols define the rules for addressing and routing data packets, delivering packets and retransmitting them when there is a delivery failure, and monitoring networks. A brief description of three key protocols follows:

■ The Internet Protocol (IP) routes packets to their proper destination. This is the core protocol that all other Internet protocols rely upon.

■ The Transmission Control Protocol (TCP) works at a higher level to ensure the reliable delivery of packets. This includes an initial packet transmission, an acknowledgment that the packet was received, and a retransmission if the packet was not received.

■ The User Datagram Protocol (UDP) is an alternative to TCP. UDP does not ensure reliable delivery. It just blasts packets across the network and hopes for the best. Thus, UDP is not slowed by the acknowledgment and retransmission mechanism of the TCP protocol. This can be a disaster if you are transmitting a document or program. However, for data types such as audio and video, the speed of the transmission is critical, and a few missing packets here and there probably won't be noticed.

Other Internet protocols, such as routing protocols, also exist in the network transport layers to ensure the effective and efficient operation of the network.

NETWORK APPLICATION LAYERS

Internet application layers consist of:

- ♦ a standard application programming interface, known as sockets; and
- ♦ a wide variety of application protocols that define a set of data formats and services.

Application programmers use the sockets interface to write programs that send and receive data to and from the network. These programs consist of statements similar to those used to read and write to a computer file system.

Software developers use the application protocols to create useful new client and server software for you and me. Some examples of these protocols are described below:

■The Lightweight Directory Access Protocol (LDAP) defines a directory services standard that applications can incorporate into the functions and features of new network software. A result is email client software that can look up addressing information in an LDAP directory server.

■Hypertext Transport Protocol (HTTP) defines the rules for formatting and transmitting Web pages in Internet TCP packets. This protocol is implemented in Web servers and Web browsers.

■The Simple Mail Transport Protocol (SMTP) defines protocols for the storage and forwarding of email. It is used by Internet mail servers.

■Real-Time Protocol (RTP) provides a mechanism for synchronizing and mixing time-based media that is transmitted across the network.

■The Real-Time Streaming Protocol (RTSP) defines a framework for setting up and managing real-time media streams.

Because the network applications layer is not dependent on the layers below, software developers are able to create new programs that can be readily deployed on a wide variety of physical networks throughout the global Internet and corporate intranets. Thus, Internet-centric applications programming is the dominant focus for most network software developers today. Almost every sort of software application you can think of is now being retrofitted or developed from scratch for Internet access capability. For example:

■The basic word processor now doubles as a Web browser and a Web page editor.

■Programs that provide access to useful CD-ROM databases are being designed with hooks to Internet information stores, thereby enabling ongoing updates.

■Email clients and servers, originally developed for proprietary network environments, have been reborn as SMTP (the Internet email transfer protocol), POP (Post Office Protocol), and IMAP (Independent Messaging Access Protocol) email systems.

■Even games are being fitted with an Internet link to enable multiplayer gaming across the Net.

The "Web-ification" of applications software is another trend. Applications previously accessible only through a specialized, proprietary interface are now being retrofitted with a Web interface. This allows global access via a consistent user interface to an ever widening variety of applications software. Examples include:

- database update and retrieval interfaces that are performed through Web-based forms;
- the development of Web interfaces for many client/server enterprise information systems;
- chat and email availability through Web pages and forms; and
- Internet application servers administered through a Web interface.

Another outcome of the move to Web-based computing is the evolution of the Web browser into a multifunction applications platform. Today's Web browser can do much more than browse the Web. Newer versions of the browsers from Netscape (Communicator) and Microsoft (Internet Explorer) include email, calendaring, and other information access and information-sharing functions.

We'll review some other important application layer protocols and standards plus digital convergence applications in Chapter 7.

IP EVERYWHERE!

The Internet is the focal point for most digital convergence technologies and applications, and it is a network that will grow and evolve with a connectedness that will continue to amaze. Eventually the Internet will be everywhere, even replacing the telephone network and most broadcast networks.

The Internet is a global conglomeration of interconnected networks. Corporate networks and regional and local Internet service provider (ISP) networks are all interconnected by the backbone infrastructure of tier one ISPs and telecommunications carriers, such as Performance Systems International, MCI/Worldcom, AT&T, and Sprint.

Each of these companies maintains its segment of the Internet by using high-bandwidth technology, usually based on fiber-optic backbones and extremely high-speed routers. Peering agreements among the major ISPs allow Internet traffic to flow between the various backbones at a series of geographically dispersed network access points (NAPs).

Most ISPs offer Web-hosting services and a variety of access options. These options range from slow modem connections for consumers on up through high-speed corporate access that primarily uses landline copper- and fiber-based links. New players, including local and regional phone companies and cable and satellite television providers, are now offering alternative high-speed access for businesses and consumers.

OBSTACLES

The current Internet is a phenomenal network, but there are two major issues that need to be addressed before it can realize its full potential as the primary network for voice, video, and data.

The Local Loop

Consumer access to the Internet is most often via dial-up modems at very slow speeds. Thankfully, though, this is beginning to change. The need for high-speed access in the local loop is being stimulated by digital convergence technologies and applications that are pushing the envelope in the use of graphics, audio, and video.

Streaming media and interactive conferencing at low bandwidths often result in garbled audio and blurry, freeze-frame video. Something as simple as downloading graphic-rich Web pages or email messages with attached files over a 28.8 Kbps modem, or even a 56 Kbps modem, can strain the patience of all but the most zealous Web-hounds. A growing number of modem users are willing to pay a premium for speedier Internet access that makes rich-media experiences not just tolerable, but downright pleasurable and much more useful.

The first adopters of high-speed last-mile technology will be small businesses and a small, but rapidly growing, group of consumers who are heavy Internet users. As the number of high-speed users and competition increases, costs will decline, leading to more widespread deployment. For many consumers, however, the cost of a PC is already prohibitive. Before high-speed Internet access really reaches the masses, we'll need to see a thin client computer or television set-top box that is bundled with high-speed access at a reasonable monthly fee.

The race is on to provide high-speed Internet access to home office users, consumers, and small businesses. The players—cable television companies, digital satellite services,

Internet service providers, global telecommunications carriers, and local and regional phone companies—have some very interesting offerings, indeed.

Cable—Cable modem service is now available in many metropolitan areas, usually through a hybrid fiber-optic and coaxial network. Fiber runs from the cable head end to a neighborhood fiber drop, and then a coaxial cable delivers the signal into consumers' homes. This service provides a high-speed access that typically offers download speeds of millions of bits per second and an upload rate of hundreds of kilobits per second. (See Chapter 3 for more details on cable TV networks and a description of the head end.)

Unfortunately, cable bandwidth is shared within a neighborhood. So, as demand for the service grows and rich-media applications proliferate, your neighbors will be using up bandwidth that could slow down your Internet access in the process. Cable companies have promised to manage the network so that as more and more neighbors get connected, users won't see a return to the World Wide Wait.

xDSL—Digital subscriber line access is now offered by some regional telephone companies, ISPs and local telecommunications carriers. This technology is the result of an earlier unsuccessful phone company effort to develop video-on-demand services. The technology developed for that effort is being fitted for Internet access. It will offer a much faster alternative to the widely available ISDN (integrated services digital network), which is the digital phone service that provides connections at 128 Kbps per line.

xDSL can run over existing copper cables, eliminating the need for telcos to implement expensive new cabling systems. Like the cable modem, it is an always-on network technology that will provide round-the-clock network access. But unlike cable access, bandwidth is not shared. An xDSL connection is a dedicated digital pipe to your home or place of work.

The first xDSL service to be widely deployed, called ADSL Lite, is a standardized version of ADSL (asynchronous digital subscriber line). It will offer download transfers at 1.5 million bits per second with return speeds at hundreds of kilobits per second.

Symmetric digital subscriber line (SDSL), another xDSL offering, enables bidirectional transfer rates that are identical. This is more commonly offered to businesses needing both high-speed egress and ingress to their piece of the Internet. A DSL technology we'll see in the future, named high-bit-rate digital subscriber line (HDSL), will offer performance in the range of tens of megabits per second.

Existing telco copper cable infrastructures can handle xDSL, but there are distance considerations that can limit performance for long runs and render some high-speed flavors of xDSL unavailable when the copper run is just too long. Thus, telcos are also beginning to implement a hybrid fiber and copper solution similar to the fiber-coaxial network model that cable companies are rolling out. The telcos are running high-speed fiber connections into the neighborhoods, where xDSL-ready copper cables will travel from the neighborhood fiber drops into consumers' homes.

Wireless—There are two types of wireless solutions that provide high-speed Internet access. One is based on space-borne satellite transmission, and the other is based on terrestrial radio waves.

Current satellite-based Internet services, such as Hughes DirecPC, use high-orbiting geostationary satellites. The satellite orbit is synchronized with the rotation of the earth, so the satellite hovers over the same spot on the planet. This option is becoming popular among rural users who don't have access to cable systems and can't get ADSL service.

This technology offers download speeds of hundreds of

kilobits per second, but it requires a landline return, typically a modem connection. It also introduces a noticeable delay, because even though the transmission is traveling at light speed, it must go quite a distance. The transmission delay and upload bottleneck effectively disable interactive applications, such as videoconferencing, that require high-speed, low-delay data transmission in both directions.

Other satellite systems, being implemented as I write this, will offer high-speed bidirectional Internet access with less delay than that of geostationary satellite systems. The most notable is the low-earth-orbiting satellite grid called Teledesic, a project backed by Bill Gates, Motorola, and others. However, these new satellite systems are faced with significant technical challenges, and it will take a couple of years before they are ready to deploy.

High-speed terrestrial wireless services are also moving closer to reality with a number of emerging options. These are based on radio wave spectrum allocated for LMDS (local multipoint distribution service) and MMDS (multichannel multipoint distribution service), plus unlicensed spectrum. These promising technologies are just getting off the ground, and it will be some time before the companies pursuing these services will be able to work out the kinks and implement access for any significant portion of the population.

Customer service is a nontechnical factor that may be an important consideration when determining which of the high-speed local loop alternatives consumers will embrace. I've seen numerous references in the trade media that suggest consumers believe the phone company can provide superior service. In my experience, it seems the reverse is true.

I live in an older neighborhood of a northeastern U.S. city, where the phone company's copper cable plant is aged. We have had no end to problems with noise on our lines. To get a second line installed for ordinary modem-based Internet access, it took two trucks—one from the installer and one from the repair crew. Getting service has been a painful experience at best. I've had a similar negative experience at Syracuse University when configuring ISDN lines for videoconferencing. On the other hand, our Time Warner cable connection was hooked up in one visit, and it's been solid as a rock.

Once we do have widespread high-speed access in consumers' homes, we'll see home networking products emerge to provide connectivity for all our digital devices. A domestic LAN will enable the whole family to access the high-speed connection simultaneously. It will also be used for telephony, and a variety of other non-PC services and devices will be connected to each other and to the fat pipe entering the home. Already, home network technology announcements are proliferating, and vendors are beginning to work out some standards for the home network, one of the last frontiers of the global digital network infrastructure.

All the high-speed local loop services described above have great promise, but the cable modem appears to have the edge as of this writing. It is already being employed in many areas, and it appears to be robust and reliable. Hopefully, xDSL will give cable access a run for its money in the short term. The overall winner of this competition will be the consumer.

Satellite or terrestrial microwave Internet access will also play an important role in the future. These options could actually displace some wired services in the long run, and wireless access will obviously offer the ultimate solution for mobile users.

End-to-End Quality of Service

The following developments might lead you to think that Internet congestion would be eliminated and that end-to-end QoS would be ensured:

■Gigabit-per-second routers are here, and terabit routers are expected soon.

■Backbone performance has increased dramatically over the past several years, from T1 speeds of 1.5 million bits per second, to T3 speeds of 45 million bits per second, on up to OC-48 at hundreds of megabits per second—with billions of bits per second the next step in the backbone progression.

■Dense wave-division multiplexing technology will yield incredible bandwidth over future fiber-optic links.

But remember, this is a packet-switched network infrastructure. Demand for bandwidth comes in spurts, and the Internet continues to find stress points. For example:

■Network access points, where major ISPs exchange traffic, are a potential source of congestion.

■Local or regional ISP networks lacking adequate bandwidth or running older, slower routers can create bottlenecks.

■Internet servers sometimes lack the computational resources or Internet connection bandwidth to keep pace with demand, thus slowing the transmission of data to network clients.

■Corporate ethernet networks using shared 10 Mbps technology can create bottlenecks due to the demands of new rich-media digital convergence applications.

I heard one network engineering expert say that, even with the fastest client Internet connection available, the current average throughput for an Internet transmission is only around 300 Kbps. For the Internet to assume the ultimate dominant role we expect of it in the emerging digital convergence architecture, it will be necessary to boost this modest end-to-end data performance. Therefore, ISPs, service providers, and LAN administrators must continue to develop the Internet infrastructure.

Part of the answer may be to focus on the new Internet network protocols that are being developed. These protocols seek to retrofit the Internet with some of the characteristics of circuit-switched networks described earlier.

One such protocol is the Resource Reservation Setup Protocol (RSVP), which is designed to guarantee the bandwidth of circuit-switched networks. If implemented throughout the Internet, RSVP protocols would ensure that the Internet can effectively support rich-media, real-time digital convergence applications, such as video streaming and Internet telephony.

When I first started working on this book, RSVP was seen as the ultimate solution to the QoS problem on the Internet. Then RSVP lost its luster, largely because of the untenable management headaches that would result if RSVP were implemented from end to end. But wait . . . RSVP has received a new life as a complement to tag switching, a new high-speed switching mechanism that the Internet Engineering Task Force is working on. (The IETF version is called multiprotocol label switching.) Stay tuned for the saga of RSVP.

ATM is a technology designed from the ground up to support the QoS guarantees that are so important for many media-rich, real-time digital convergence applications, but it has been relegated to the role of backbone technology. Implementing ATM end to end is just too costly, especially when compared to the costs of incremental enhancements to bread-and-butter ethernet technology.

A few years ago, the hype was that ATM was the solution to all our networking problems. Unfortunately, ATM has fallen far short of the mark.

Several other schemes are now being developed to improve Internet quality of service. For example:

■Network switches are being fitted with proprietary ASICs, which can perform routing and traffic prioritization. This will ensure adequate bandwidth for specific real-time, media-rich applications, such as videoconferencing.

■Caching servers are being deployed in edge networks. Once someone in your locale retrieves an Internet resource, other users can retrieve it from the cache server rather than retrieving it again across the Internet.

■A scheme for differentiating network traffic is being developed. Classes of data traffic are created that can be mapped onto different service levels of an ATM network.

■A new version of the Internet Protocol, called IP version 6, promises improved QoS features.

■Adding excess network capacity to portions of the network, or overprovisioning, is being pursued to eliminate bottlenecks. Upgrading desktop connections to switched 100 Mbps ethernet, for example, will ensure that streaming video plays flawlessly across the LAN.

By the time you read this, new quality of service approaches will have emerged, and one or more of those described above may be placed on the back burner by the industry. QoS continues to command the attention of the top network engineers in the business. Additionally, because quality of service is one of the keys to the future of the Internet and digital convergence, QoS initiatives are receiving a massive infusion of research and development dollars.

DIGITAL MULTIMEDIA

For decades, computers have made it easy to manipulate words and numbers. Now it is also easy to create, edit, and store images, sounds, animations, and video, and then integrate these media with each other and with words and numbers. The results form the basis of content and interactions that are shared throughout the global network via the technologies of digital convergence.

In Chapter 3, we briefly reviewed digital data representations for a variety of media types and the methods of digitizing these media (capturing). We also discussed the data volume challenges presented by rich-media types, especially video. In this chapter, I'll describe in detail some of the hardware and software technologies for capturing, editing, and integrating image, sound, video, and other digital media. Then a brief discussion of some of the tools you can use to integrate digital media will be followed by an introduction to media compression.

Many of the multimedia tools and technologies discussed in this chapter were not developed as network-centric technologies, though almost all now have Internet hooks. Most have been around for some time. In the next chapter, I will cover the newer digital media technologies that have been developed specifically for the network environment. These are among the most interesting and promising digital convergence technologies.

Digital media technologies range from simple low-cost technologies for knowledge workers and consumers to high-end technologies for media professionals, such as graphic designers, photographers, video producers, and audio engineers.

Professionals use high-end digital multimedia technologies to create and integrate stunning high-resolution images, complex musical ensembles, and broadcast-quality video, video animations, and special affects. Although these technologies are complex and costly, they continue to evolve, enabling creative pros to further extend the boundaries of high-quality media. You encounter the results of advanced digital media manipulation all the time on radio, on television, in glossy magazines, and, of course, on the Web.

Like most digital technologies, lower-end multimedia tools have increased dramatically in functionality, capability, and ease of use over the past few years. At the same time, decreasing prices have been almost as dramatic. The gap between high-end and low-end tools is narrowing, and the difference between quality media and substandard media is now more often tied to the quality of application rather than the quality of the tool.

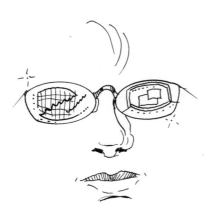

In keeping with the emphasis of this book on the ability of new technology to empower individuals and workgroups, I'll focus on the lower-end technologies. These tools are easy to learn and use, and they are available for standard desktop computers at a reasonable cost.

IMAGES

SCANNERS

The image scanner is the most commonly used tool for capturing digital images. Scanners vary widely in quality and cost, from inexpensive handheld document scanners to expensive film scanners used by photographers and publishing service bureaus. Factors that usually drive scanner purchase decisions include capture resolution (dots per inch as well as bit depth for color resolution), types and dimensions of material that can be scanned, and bundled software.

Here's a quick look at two types of inexpensive scanners frequently used by individuals and workgroups.

The most popular scanner is the flatbed scanner. Similar to an office photocopy machine, it features a glass surface that you lay your image on. A mechanism below the glass moves across the image, shining light on it. A series of mirrors focuses the reflected light on a CCD (charge-coupled device) where the light intensity of each pixel is converted to an analog voltage and then digitized.

Even inexpensive flatbed scanners can produce an image of decent quality. Also, they can accept a wide range of input media, including books, magazines, and even some 3D objects. Flatbed scanners are available in consumer-grade models that provide good-quality scans with a resolution of at least 600 x 1200 dots per inch in 24-bit color. More expensive, but still reasonably priced, professional models will do much higher resolution scanning at a higher bit depth. The flatbed scanner has become firmly established as the image capture workhorse for individuals and workgroups.

The sheet-fed scanner is another type of inexpensive scanner. Sheets of paper are fed through the scanner, and the capture mechanism is fixed, as it is on a fax machine.

These scanners are often used by the mobile worker needing to scan images or text on the go. Compact, lightweight sheet-fed scanners are a great option in these circumstances. The sheet-fed scanner is also frequently found in the home office environment, where multifunction machines can scan, fax, and print. Although these scanners are convenient, they produce lower-quality images than flatbed scanners. Also, input media is limited because whatever you want to scan must fit through the sheet-feeder.

The original cover art for this book is an acrylic painting on canvas. When the artwork was created, I decided to scan a copy for possible future use (I share the copyright with my publisher). If all I had was a sheet-fed scanner, I'd have been out of luck. Instead, I used a Umax flatbed scanner available at my workplace, and it did an excellent job of capturing Freddy's fine work.

A good flatbed scanner can capture a scanned image directly from within an image editing software, such as Adobe Photoshop, by using a driver that allows the image editor to take control of the scanner. Software bundled with a good flatbed scanner will also let you set bit depth and pixel resolution for each scan. This is important because different situations require different scanner settings. For example:

■When scanning photos or graphics from a magazine or some other printed source, it is sometimes necessary to fiddle with scan resolution to get a decent image. The printing process lays down tiny dots of cyan, magenta, yellow, and black ink. These print dots can be poorly aligned (with respect to pixel capture) at some scanning resolutions, and thus create what looks like a plaid pattern over the image.

■If you want to capture your signature, you would choose a line-art scan that uses only black and white for all pixels.

■Graphics for the Web will appear on computer monitors at only 72 dots per inch, so a modest scan resolution of 150 dots per inch with full 24-bit color is appropriate.

Getting good-quality scanned images is a bit of an art, and those who do a lot of scanning will end up spending considerable time learning the tricks that ensure quality results.

DIGITAL CAMERAS

Digital cameras offer another useful option for creating digital images. Just point and click as you would with a film camera, and the image in the camera lens is captured directly in digital format by using the same CCD technology found in scanners.

Pictures are stored temporarily in the camera's digital picture memory. If the memory is internal to the camera, you will need to connect the camera to a serial or USB (universal serial bus) port to download the pictures. If the pictures are stored on a flash memory card or floppy disk (Sony cameras use a floppy), you simply remove the card, or disk, and pop it into your computer.

The maximum number of pictures you can shoot before downloading to a PC depends on the resolution of the images you shoot and the size of the digital picture memory store. Most cameras take pictures at two resolution settings, one high and one low. The low-resolution setting obviously uses less memory than the high-resolution setting, but the high-resolution setting ensures quality results.

When I first started looking into digital cameras a couple of years ago, 640 x 480 pixels was fairly standard. This resolution is far inferior to the resolution you achieve with standard photographic film media. Cameras have now become available that offer resolutions of 1024 x 768 pixels and higher. Some of these high-resolution megapixel cameras begin to approach the picture quality of film-based cameras.

Of course, quality is just one factor. Digital cameras have other features that conventional cameras lack. In many applications, the convenience of having the image immediately available in a digital format is a big plus. For example, when taking pictures for a Web site, the digital camera is an attractive tool. Image quality is already limited by network bandwidth and the resolution of your computer monitor. You can take dozens of pictures, quickly and easily download them to your PC, and then put them up on the Web where they are immediately accessible around the globe.

The School of Management owns a few inexpensive

digital cameras that are used to take snapshots at alumni gatherings and other school events. At the conclusion of the event, we quickly download the pictures to a PC, pop the best ones onto some Web pages, save those pages on our Web server, and set up a link from the news and features section of our Web site. This lets us share the event with the entire university as well as prospective students, parents, and alumni.

High-end digital cameras are also used by professional photographers as circumstances dictate. For example, a newspaper photographer can shoot some pictures on the scene of a late-breaking news event and quickly upload them to the newspaper office. In this way, they can be immediately incorporated into the latest edition of the evening paper.

Analog film cameras still offer a decided advantage for many applications. For example, digital cameras can't produce action shots at the same level of quality as the film-based cameras that are used for sports and other high-action situations. Also, for extremely high-quality photography, digital cameras are far from challenging the price performance of the conventional camera.

The price of digital cameras will decrease over time as quality, functionality, and capacity increase. Digital cameras have already found a place in niche applications, such as the automobile insurance and residential realty businesses. They are a useful tool for a variety of business professionals and consumers, and, eventually, we will see digital cameras displace film cameras in most business applications. Over time, the digital camera will also become a more viable option for many professional photographers, who currently remain heavy users of silver-halide film media.

PhotoCD AND PhotoNet

An easy and inexpensive option for converting film-based images to digital format is Kodak's PhotoCD service, available through your local film developer. This service converts film or negatives to a digital format and returns them to you on CD-ROM. A variety of formats is offered, including a high-resolution version that is suitable for many publishing applications.

Kodak has another similar service, called PhotoNet, that converts your images to a digital format and makes them available on the Internet. To access and download the images, you use a Kodak-supplied password. The password can be shared with business colleagues, friends, and family, who may have the need or desire to check out your evolving digital photo repository.

If you want to explore the world of digital images before laying out hard cash for a digital camera or scanner, you should investigate one of these services by using your own snapshots. PhotoCD and PhotoNet are also useful if you want a digital version of archive photos, provided you still have your negatives.

IMAGE FORMATS

The three most common image formats for desktop computers are:

- ♦ BMP (bitmap), developed and implemented for Windows-based graphical images;
- ♦ TIFF (tagged image file format), developed by Aldus (a major desktop publishing and multimedia software vendor) for scanned images; and
- ♦ PICT, a graphics standard developed for the Macintosh.

Most scanning software and image editing software includes an option to open and save images in these standard formats. GIF (graphics interchange format) and JPG, or JPEG (Joint Photographic Experts Group), are two other very common image formats. They are used primarily for network access, and they will be covered in the next chapter.

EDITING AND CREATING IMAGES

Adobe Photoshop is a software program that has set the standard for digital image editing. It enables incredible control and creativity, and it includes a slew of tools and filters to manipulate images that go well beyond what you might expect. Advanced tools, such as the "magic wand" that lets you select only that portion of the image that you want to manipulate, plus precise color control can produce powerful effects.

By using a digital image editor, an image that has been scanned or captured with a digital camera can be embellished with additional visual elements. For example, you can quickly and easily:

♦ use paintbrushes, pens, and even an airbrush to digitally paint and draw;
♦ select a portion of an image and fill it with color;
♦ add shading effects and drop shadows; and
♦ include stylistic text elements.

You've surely seen many images that have been created from scratch or embellished with these visual elements. These images appear in advertising, educational materials, and, of course, on Web sites.

Images have become an integral part of the Web experience. Web graphics can make a Web site easier to use and, at the same time, you are communicating with your users in a subtle, but very powerful, way. Graphics may seem like a frill to some, but the effective use of images adds a useful dimension to the Web experience.

Photoshop is a complex program that is challenging to learn, but the results can be worth the effort. I spent a couple of months trying to learn this package by reading books, searching the Web for tips and tricks, and trial and error. I never really got the hang of it until I attended a daylong Photoshop training session. There, I received a clear explanation of the basics of how this tool worked and learned a boatload of tricks. Since the training, Photoshop has become a very useful tool for me. I'm not all that artistically inclined, but I've amazed myself at what I can do.

Recently, I used Photoshop to create graphics for a prototype of a distance-learning Web site. The tool allowed me to quickly and easily fashion graphics that gave the site a professional and engaging look and feel. There was minimal functionality in the prototype, but the graphical front end was very useful for communicating the vision and ultimate purpose of the prospective site.

Although Photoshop is the original digital image workhorse, some other capable image editors, such as Corel PhotoPaint, offer serious competition. There are also a number of low-end digital image editors for straightforward consumer and business applications. These include Microsoft Picture It and MGI PhotoSuite.

When using an image editor to create or edit images, you are altering the pixel information directly. It is a lot like painting with a brush on canvas. The images thus created and edited are called bitmapped images.

A drawing, or illustration, tool is another way of creating digital imagery, but a different model is used to represent the visual elements that comprise an image. Instead of creating a canvas of pixels, the drawing tool creates and edits shape descriptions that are based on vector mathematics. CorelDraw and Adobe Illustrator are two popular vector-based drawing packages.

Objects created by vector-based drawing tools tend to have sharper, cleaner edges than those of bitmapped images. The size of a vector object is easily altered, and vector drawings are more compact than bitmapped images because vectors provide a very compact representation of the visual imagery.

Digital 3D (three dimensional) imagery is another graphical genre that is gaining popularity. There is an increasing number of tools for both creating 3D images from scratch and converting 2D images to a 3D format. This is really very cool, and some predict that 3D imagery will surface as an important visual medium in the future.

There will be some useful applications of this technology, certainly, but the added complexity of creating quality 3D media and applying that imagery in useful ways may relegate this technology to niche applications. A technical reality that will slow adoption is the voluminous size of 3D images and the significant processing they require. Interactive gaming is one realm where 3D imagery has taken off, but only serious gamers are up to the task of installing the special 3D video card that is needed to fully experience 3D gaming.

AUDIO

For many years, Macintosh computers have shipped with built-in sound and microphones, while IBM-compatible PCs lacked this feature. PC users who wanted sound had to add the hardware and software after purchase. Now, almost every PC for the consumer market comes out of the box with a sound card installed. The 16-bit sound card that is now standard on most PCs can easily capture sound in a high-fidelity format.

Most business computers also come with a sound card, though there are still some models that do not. Some businesses see the sound card as a frill that will only succeed in diverting employees from real work, a rather shortsighted view in my opinion.

AUDIO FORMATS

Like digital images, sound has its own standard digital file formats. The standard Windows format is the WAV (waveform) file, and it is based on the numeric values generated during sampling (described in Chapter 3). For the Macintosh, the audio interchange file format (AIFF) is standard. Some sound-editing software can handle only one format or the other, although the more sophisticated and capable software can combine and convert a variety of formats.

Another format, called MIDI (musical instrument digital interface), offers an alternative method of storing sounds. A MIDI file consists of a set of computer instructions that are used to synthesize the MIDI sound when it is executed by a MIDI-compatible device. Older MIDI-capable sound cards use a technique called FM synthesis to synthesize MIDI sounds, while newer sound cards use a superior technique called wavetable synthesis.

A set of standard MIDI "instruments" is built into MIDI sound cards. You can also create your own MIDI instruments by capturing sounds and converting them to MIDI format. This is done by using a process known as sampling. It is similar to the sampling that occurs when converting analog sounds to digital format, except the resulting analog wave form is converted to MIDI instructions. MIDI instruments don't have to be instruments at all, of course. A MIDI instrument can be a human voice, a gunshot, or the honk of a horn.

A variety of MIDI devices, such as music keyboards and drum machines, can be combined to create  sophisticated electronic sound systems. These systems can sample sounds to create new MIDI instruments or to create and compose complete MIDI musical works. The end results are saved as MIDI or WAV files, or output to analog recording devices.

EDITING AND CREATING AUDIO

Basic software for editing captured sounds is inexpensive, easy to use, and very capable. For example, when I purchased a Soundblaster sound card for my home PC a couple of years ago, it shipped with Creative Labs' Creative Wave Studio. This simple tool easily captures sound from multiple sound sources—a music CD in the computer's CD-ROM drive, a microphone, or a tape or CD player connected to the line-in connector on the sound card. Using the same simple software to edit the resulting WAV file, I could cut and paste sounds, add fade-in and fade-out effects, and add special effects such as echo.

More sophisticated WAV editors, such as Sound Forge or CoolEdit, let you do more with your sound file. You can add a wider variety of effects to your sounds, and you can also selectively change the volume of different frequency ranges. This enables you to eliminate background noise, reduce the volume of sounds that dominate unnecessarily, and boost the sound level of other frequencies, thereby ensuring a high-quality finished product.

MIDI software includes some advanced packages.

Cakewalk Pro Audio, an industry standard audio software tool, lets you compose and edit MIDI works in multiple tracks. You can even edit your music using an electronic musical score. E-MU Systems has come out with a complete sound studio bundle that includes a MIDI sound card, a set of connectors for musical instruments and recording devices that you install in an open drive bay, and software designed for digital audio pros.

MIDI is a fascinating medium for hobbyists and a powerful tool for digitally inclined musicians, but MIDI technology tends to be complex and expensive. Many of us are looking for something that is simpler, less expensive, and easier to use.

A new genre of easy-to-use digital music software is now emerging that offers limited functionality, yet it is sufficient to create background music for a Web page or a business video. For example, I've downloaded a package from the Internet, called Making Waves, that allows you to easily compose simple music by using 400 or so canned WAV sounds. You can create and add your own WAV sounds as well. This tool makes it possible to create some interesting background sounds with only a modest investment of time and effort.

Mixman Studio is another package that uses canned sounds to compose music. Mixman allows you to add effects to your music, such as panning from one stereo channel to another, and it includes song templates to help you get started. Your finished composition can then be exported as an MP3 file. (We will cover MP3 in the next chapter.)

The quality of the music you create with these simple tools may be called into question by real musicians, but this technology is promising for those of us who have a creative bent and are willing to experiment. If you are able to generate some reasonable sounds, the resulting files can be integrated easily with other digital media.

VIDEO

VIDEO CAPTURE TECHNOLOGIES

Most desktop video capture entails connecting an analog video camera or video recording device to a digital capture card in your PC. A wide variety of PC video capture cards are now available, offering different capabilities and different price points.

The least-expensive cards have significant limitations, such as a maximum capture rate that is far below television's 30 frames per second or a strict limit on the size of the image you can capture. Most low-end video cards capture video without sound. You must use your sound card to capture the audio.

I happen to own two low-end video capture cards, an Intel Video Recorder Pro and a Pinnacle MiroVIDEO DRX . These cards are appropriate for computer-based projects such as creating a multimedia CD-ROM or an Internet streaming video. Like many low-end capture cards, however, they are not adequate for even VHS-quality video.

One of the most significant parameters for video capture is frame rate. Anything below 15 frames per second begins to look choppy. Unfortunately, some low-end video capture cards struggle to achieve reasonable frame rates.

Some low-end cards also limit the pixel dimensions of your video image. In most cases, a larger image size is desirable. The usual starting point is 320 x 240 pixels, and 640 x 480 pixels is considered full-screen digital video. A smaller image size, say 160 x 120 pixels, is often used for some applications, such as a talking head video in a multimedia CD-ROM or in a Web video. Under these circumstances, the limitations of the capture card aren't an issue.

Today's video monitors are typically set for a resolution

of 800 x 600 pixels, so video images at 160 x 120 pixels appear very small. This is called "postage stamp" video.

More expensive cards can capture video in a format suitable for VHS quality, at minimum. These cards also include connectors for outputting your edited video directly to a videotape deck.

The combination of two new video technologies is now poised to overtake the desktop video market. DV is a digital video capture standard that was developed by a consortium of video product manufacturers, and firewire is the high-speed serial bus technology that was described in Chapter 4. DV has been used in several new digital video cameras, and firewire is being implemented in both DV cameras and desktop PCs.

DV video cameras are available at a reasonable cost, and they offer a picture quality clearly superior to that of a consumer-grade VHS or 8mm video camera. Once you've shot some video and want to edit, you simply connect the camera to a PC, via firewire, and download the digital video from the camera's digital tape. This simple digital file download is part of an all-digital solution designed to prevent the loss of quality that usually occurs when dealing with analog media.

One way I try to keep up on desktop video is to check out the *Desktop Video Handbook* that the Videoguys maintain (*http://www.videoguys.com*). In their latest version, the Videoguys claimed that they're now selling more DV cameras and firewire add-in cards than analog-to-digital capture technology. At this point, the Sony Vaio is the only Wintel computer that ships with a firewire connector (Apple's G3 includes firewire), and it is positioned as a digital video workstation. I expect (and hope) that other PC manufacturers will soon equip high-end computers with firewire.

Digital Video Formats

Two long-standing desktop computer video file formats are AVI (audio video interleaved) and Quicktime. AVI is the standard video format for Windows. The Windows media player will play any AVI file, and MS Office lets you insert AVI files into Word, Excel, and PowerPoint files.

Quicktime is the standard for the Macintosh computer, and the MacOS has built-in tools for viewing Quicktime video. Quicktime for Windows can be installed on any Windows desktop, so Wintel users can also access Quicktime video.

These two formats are the ones you most often deal with when capturing and editing low-end digital video for the Web. Listed below are a few other common digital video formats.

- DV is the relatively new video format described in the previous section. This format will play an important role in the future of desktop digital video.
- Motion-JPEG (MJPEG) is often used for professional work as it is a good editing format. This high-quality format uses JPEG compression, which we will cover in the next chapter.
- MPEG (also covered in the next chapter) is used for CD-ROM video and for satellite television. MPEG is a high-quality compressed video format, but it is not a good editing format.

EDITING DIGITAL VIDEO

Inexpensive software for editing video is available for standard PC and Macintosh desktop computers. Many low-end video capture cards ship with a video editing package, usually either Adobe Premier or Ulead Media Studio Pro. These are nonlinear video editors that enable you to work with multiple video and audio tracks. For example, you can easily:

◆ trim the various video clips that you'll be inserting into your video;

◆ set up transitions between clips;

◆ add a music or narration track (or both);

◆ overlay your video with stylized text elements;

◆ insert static full-screen graphic images in lieu of video; and

◆ superimpose graphics over video.

Although very capable nonlinear video editing packages, such as Premier, will dominate the low-end video realm, there are packages that are even simpler to use. They are also more limited. When I purchased my miroVIDEO DRX capture card a little over a year ago, it shipped with an extremely easy-to-use video editing software called MGI Videowave.

The tools for producing quality video on standard desktop computers are now available at a very reasonable cost. Like every other media technology, they continue to increase in quality and functionality while decreasing in price. This dovetails nicely with rapidly evolving digital convergence technologies, such as streaming media. Video is rapidly becoming an integral part of the digital media experience.

THIRD-PARTY MEDIA

A great deal of digital media is available at your fingertips, and it is an attractive option for many multimedia projects. For example:

■Microsoft Office comes with clip-art libraries and sound effects that you can use to enhance your presentations.

■The Web has all kinds of sites that offer free downloads of graphic images, sound effects, MIDI music, and animations. These can all be easily incorporated into a multimedia resource. Copyrights may restrict the use of some media, so be careful when using media developed by others.

■Your CD-ROM or DVD drive is another potential source of digital media. For a fee, many outfits will send you disks packed with sound clips, images, video clips, and animations. Pop these into your computer, and you've got yourself a useful media library that is fully integrated with the creative tools of your desktop computer.

Why spend time and energy creating audio and video that may play only a small part in your project if someone has already created something you can get inexpensively or free?

PUTTING IT ALL TOGETHER

Creating lovely images, juicy sound tracks, or great video is just the beginning for media that is digital. All these media can be integrated to create new media that offers far more than conventional analog photography, audio recording, and video. These new media can range from fairly straightforward textual works with integrated images to full-fledged multimedia experiences that include hyperlinked images, audio, and video with special effects.

Authoring is the term used to describe the process of creating an interactive experience that incorporates multiple media.

One of the most common, but often overlooked, authoring environments is the standard office productivity suite. Microsoft Office is the runaway winner in this market. MS Office makes it easy to integrate text with images, video, and sounds in electronic documents, electronic presentations, and spreadsheets. Pull down the Word, Excel, or PowerPoint "Insert" menu, specify an image you want to include, and there it is. You can easily resize the image within the document to fit the flow of the content you're developing. The same "Insert" menu can be used to add video or sound.

Two much more capable authoring tools are Macromedia Director and Asymmetric Toolbook. Director can be used to create a hyperlinked, time-based multimedia experience. In the hands of a pro, it is most often used to create rich and sophisticated electronic advertising media, learning environments, and marketing resources.

Toolbook enables the creation of rich hyperlinked media resources, and it is most often used to create interactive learning environments and training materials.

Multimedia authoring software packages, such as MS Office, Director, and Toolbook, were originally developed to create multimedia that would be delivered directly from a desktop disk or CD-ROM. These packages were not tuned for network access. Eventually, however, these packages were extended so that the resulting multimedia could be converted to a format for network access. Now, these and other authoring tools are being retrofitted with technology that allows you to develop a project for the Web and save it directly to the Web.

COMPRESSION

Recall the data volume problem discussed in Chapter 3, and you will remember that high-quality images, audio, and video generate enormous amounts of data. This fact has stimulated the development of a number of innovative compression techniques and technologies that minimize the amount of data required to digitally represent rich media.

Some of the first digital media compression technologies for desktop computers were developed to compress data that needed to be stored and delivered directly from local storage devices (hard drive or CD-ROM). Thus, AVI and Quicktime video formats (using Indeo and Cinepak compression, respectively) were developed to reduce the data storage requirements of digital video, but they were designed for media delivery only from hard disk or CD-ROM.

In the next chapter, we'll examine in detail a few of the important image, audio, and video compression technologies that have been designed for network transmission of digital media. Some have emerged as important digital convergence technologies. In this chapter, we'll stick to an introduction of compression concepts, so you can gain a sense of how these technologies work.

Compression can be lossless, meaning that the entire original media object or data file can be completely reproduced from compressed form. Lossless compression is most often used for documents, programs, and other data files, where the loss of data would corrupt the information it represents and render it useless. If you've ever used WinZip to create or extract a Zip archive consisting of one or more computer files, you've used a lossless compression technology. Unfortunately, lossless compression is unable to achieve the really sizable reductions in data volume that are required for network-centric rich-media applications.

Lossy compression technology uses techniques that actually discard some of the original data. The loss of a few pixels or some sound data isn't critical to audio, video, or graphic images. This is because the human eye and ear are somewhat forgiving when interpreting the end result. Lossy compression can achieve much greater compression gains than lossless techniques.

Compression results are expressed as ratios. A lossless compression technology applied to a document or program file might be able to achieve a 3:1, or even a 10:1, compression ratio, but a lossy compression technology applied to video might routinely achieve a ratio of 100:1.

Compression technology is the application of computerized procedures, called algorithms, that reduce the number of bits required to represent a given media object. An algorithm encodes the media during compression, and an inverse algorithm decodes the information to reproduce the original. Because compression technologies use algorithms to encode and then decode the media, these technologies are often called codecs, and compression is often referred to as encoding. The following examples illustrate how compression is applied.

■Many images have significant amounts of space that use the same color. Rather than store complete information for every pixel, an image compression algorithm might store the value of only the first pixel of a certain color plus the number of subsequent pixels that also use that color.

■Some videos, such as a talking head video, have significant amounts of static imagery from frame to frame. A video compression algorithm can reduce the data required to represent video frames by storing the frame differences rather than capturing all the pixels for each frame.

■An audio compression algorithm may set a minimum threshold sound level, forcing silence below this level. It can then store a single number to keep track of the duration of silence rather than including all the digital samples for silent periods.

Compression algorithms use many such tricks to reduce data storage for rich media.

Now let's move on to one of the most exciting parts of this book: a focused review and analysis of today's rapidly emerging digital convergence technologies and applications.

7

DIGITAL CONVERGENCE TECHNOLOGIES

Built from a combination of computing, communications, and digital media technologies, digital convergence technologies offer us powerful new tools for sharing information and interacting with one another.

Digital convergence technologies obliterate barriers of distance and time, providing anywhere, anytime communication and information sharing.

The interactions that these technologies enable are incredibly varied. They range from real-time one-to-one communications to globally accessible electronic resources that reach mass audiences on demand. These technologies also integrate all digital media types. Indeed, one of the most powerful aspects of the digital convergence phenomenon is that these technologies can be used to combine interactions and media in so many different ways, thus producing innovative mechanisms, tools, and information resources.

The creative among us will recognize the power and flexibility of these new tools and become the leaders of this emerging technological era. By exploring and exploiting digital convergence technologies, new ways for us to interact, communicate, collaborate, and share information will be discovered.

In this chapter, I will introduce several digital convergence technologies. As I do, you will begin to see how the combination of characteristics I've just described is beginning to play out. We'll start by discussing media compression and multimedia frameworks, two important underlying technologies that enable rich-media applications. Then we'll take a look at the World Wide Web, which is the most prominent digital convergence technology to date.

COMPRESSION TECHNOLOGY FOR THE NETWORK

The challenge of how to handle large volumes of data was outlined in Chapter 3, and, in the last chapter, I introduced the basic concepts of compression technology for digital media. As the trend toward digital convergence has gained momentum, a new genre of compression technology has sprung up that facilitates efficient transmission of various media across the digital network infrastructure.

IMAGE COMPRESSION

GIF (graphics interchange format) and JPEG (Joint Photographic Experts Group) are two image compression technologies that can dramatically reduce the size of graphic images while still retaining reasonable quality. These technologies are standard for images on the World Wide Web, and most graphics programs now include options to save images in both of these formats.

GIF is a lossless compression technology that works well for diagrams, logos, and other images. It is especially good for those images having few colors or significant portions of a single color. Before the Internet became popular, GIF was developed to compress images downloaded via the CompuServe information network.

GIF technology has evolved to include the animated GIF. This file contains a set of GIF images that are displayed in succession to create an animation effect, and it is commonly used for Web advertising.

JPEG is a lossy compression technology that allows the use of many colors. When applied to photographic images, it typically produces a higher-quality result than GIF compression

PNG (portable network graphics) is a relatively new digital image compression standard of the World Wide Web Consortium (W3C). It includes the best of both GIF and JPEG, and PNG is also royalty free. This is a significant point. Because GIF compression employs a technology patented by Unisys, CompuServe and Unisys declared in 1995 that implementing GIF in applications software would require a royalty payment. PNG is now supported in many graphics packages and in the newest browsers from Netscape and Microsoft. You can expect PNG to slowly become a mainstream image compression format as the use of older non-PNG-compatible software declines.

AUDIO AND VIDEO COMPRESSION

Audio and video compression for the network is a mix of standards-based and proprietary technologies.

The International Telecommunications Union (ITU) is a global standards organization historically driven by the needs of national and/or international telephone companies. As the digital convergence phenomenon takes shape, the ITU is re-defining its role and stepping in to develop key standards. A series of audio compression standards developed by the ITU includes:

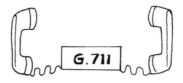

■G.711—This digital audio compression standard is for transmission over network connections at 48 to 64 Kbps. It is the standard used for the digital component of today's circuit-switched phone network.

■G.728—This is an ITU compression standard for audio running at low bit rates (16 Kbps). It is implemented in most ISDN- and packet-based videoconferencing systems.

■G.723—For audio at even lower bit rates (5.3 and 6.5 Kbps), this standard is used for modem-to-modem videoconferencing over plain old telephone circuits and for audio/videoconferencing over low-speed packet-switched network connections.

The International Telecommunications Union has also developed video compression standards, primarily for videoconferencing, that include:

■H.261—This video compression standard supports ISDN-based videoconferencing.

■H.263—For video compression, this standard is designed for videoconferencing over packet networks, such as the Internet.

The Motion Picture Experts Group (MPEG), a committee of the International Standards Organization (ISO), has coordinated a number of important audio/video compression standards. MPEG-1 was developed for motion video over bandwidths up to 1.5 Mbps. MPEG-2 was developed for higher-bandwidth transmissions, including high definition television (HDTV) broadcasts.

These technologies use sophisticated interframe compression techniques that maximize quality while minimizing decompression processing at the client. A new technology that is really a multimedia framework, MPEG-4, is described in the next section.

The MPEG-1 standard includes MPEG Layer 3, often referred to as MP3, or MPEG-3. This audio compression format has become popular for Internet transmission and the storage of digital music. MP3 produces highly compressed music files that near the quality of CDs. You can download MP3 audio to your desktop PC from the Internet and play it there, or you can create MP3 recordings on removable media to play in a portable MP3 player, such as the Diamond Rio.

MP3 has created quite a stir in the music recording industry because it enables unscrupulous individuals to easily distribute copyrighted works illegally. On the other hand, it has empowered musicians who want to record and disseminate their music directly. Many up-and-coming artists (and some well-known artists, such as Public Enemy) have published their music directly on the Web using MP3, often to the chagrin of music recording industry executives. This is a good example of the powerful effects of digital convergence. It can create unique opportunities for creative minds and turn a stable, long-standing industry on its ear in the process.

VDONet, Real Networks, and other technology innovators have developed nonstandard, proprietary audio and video compression technologies. These efforts have been driven by the inability of existing ITU and MPEG compression standards to efficiently support audio and video applications on congested packet-switched networks (the Internet) and at very low bit rates (modem connections). Unfortunately, proprietary compression technology precludes interoperability. The media player of one vendor can't decode the media stream generated by another vendor's proprietary encoder.

WHAT ABOUT MOTION JPEG?

An MJPEG video is essentially a series of time-based JPEG image frames stored in a digital file. Because the format uses no interframe compression, MJPEG video can be edited freely. This format is often used for full-screen professional video projects with picture formats of at least 640 x 480 pixels. However, MJPEG can't achieve the compression gains of some other formats, such as MPEG-2, which is designed for network transmission of high-quality video.

The MiroVIDEO DRX video capture card offers the option to store video in MJPEG format. Although I own this card, I never use MJPEG. Mostly I'm capturing video for the Web, where full-screen, high-quality video can't be used. Besides, I only have enough disk space on my home computer to store a couple of minutes of MJPEG video. AVI is fine for what I want to do.

MULTIMEDIA FRAMEWORKS

Multimedia frameworks—the technology that enables you to integrate multiple media—now exist that provide for efficient streaming of multiple media across the Internet and corporate intranets. These media are then decoded at the client, where there is a rich-media user interaction.

Earlier multimedia frameworks have been limited and inflexible. For example:

- In its original incarnation, Apple's Quicktime was a powerful framework for integrating digital media. Unfortunately, it was not adaptable to network transmission because it had been designed for local delivery from disk or CD-ROM.
- Hypertext Markup Language (HTML), the language of the Web, requires many extensions to support the creative media integration and interaction that is now the norm.

The new generation of multimedia framework technologies is still largely unproven, but it will be very important as the move toward digital convergence gains momentum in the next few years. These frameworks are all rapidly evolving, and each is being positioned as a standard. It is too early, however, to tell which of these standards will emerge to dominate mainstream digital media applications.

Extensible Markup Language (XML) is a language standardized by the World Wide Web Consortium (W3C) to create self-describing, multimedia interactive documents. XML is touted primarily for its ability to enable electronic commerce and business information sharing. It will also be used as a foundation for network-based, interactive rich-media applications. XML is viewed by many as the next big thing in the evolution of the Internet and the Web, and it will be a part of many new digital convergence technologies. For example:

■ The Precision Graphics Markup Language (PGML) and Vector Markup Language (VML) are two proposed XML-based languages for vector graphics on the Web.

■ The next version of HTML will be based on XML, and it will include new markup tags for handling a wider variety of media types.

■ MS Office 2000 supports the XML file format.

Microsoft's Advanced Streaming Format (ASF), rooted in Microsoft's AVI technology, is a specification for a network media "container." ASF is designed to carry a wide variety of media formats that have been compressed using many different technologies, and it can run over the top of a variety of network protocols. This technology has already been implemented in both Microsoft's NetShow Services (a media server technology that is now part of Windows NT Server) and the Internet Explorer Web browser.

Apple's Quicktime is a full-fledged network-aware digital media framework. Evolving from a framework that edited and integrated only locally stored digital media, it is now a comprehensive framework that includes technology for the network transmission of digital media. Quicktime will be useful to software application developers as well as content developers.

MPEG-4 is a new media framework standard that was developed by the Motion Picture Experts Group. MPEG-4 enables streaming of multiple interactive media objects over a variety of bandwidths. Unlike MPEG-1 and MPEG-2, users will have the ability to interact with MPEG-4 media and select only those media objects that they wish to see or hear.

MPEG-4 will also support synthetic media types, such as vector graphics and animations, in their native format.

Synchronized Multimedia Integration Language (SMIL), a standard of the W3C, is used to integrate streaming text, audio, images, and video.

SMIL (pronounced smile) has been implemented in the latest release of Real Networks' streaming media technology. (For more on Real Networks' technology, see "Internet Streaming Media" below.) I used Real Network's implementation to create an integrated audio, text, image, and video presentation, and it worked beautifully. However, specifying the timing for the various streams was tedious. I look forward to new SMIL editors that will automatically generate SMIL statements.

The combination of Macromedia Director and Shockwave brings Macromedia's powerful multimedia authoring framework to the Web. (Director is described in Chapter 6.) Director content is "shocked" for Internet delivery in a process that converts it into a form suitable for Internet access, and Shockwave is the client software required to access this content via the Web. Shockwave is now being bundled with every preinstalled copy of Windows 98. Although not a standards-based multimedia framework, the combination of Director and Shockwave has already been instrumental in bringing Internet multimedia to a new level, and there is a horde of professional multimedia developers behind this technology.

These multimedia frameworks enable new types of media integration, access, and interaction. Unfortunately, the evolution of these frameworks is a work in progress that is really quite confusing. Consider the following:

- MPEG-4 is based on the Quicktime file format;

- ◆ Microsoft NetShow Services streams MPEG-4 files in ASF streams; and
- ◆ SMIL is an application of XML.

However, this is technology to keep an eye on. One or more of these frameworks will rise up to provide a standard and stable platform for the deployment of integrated multimedia content and services. Once that begins to take shape, you can expect to see new tools emerge that will empower individuals, entrepreneurs, and corporate workgroups to more aggressively explore integrated multimedia resources and applications on the Net.

THE WORLD WIDE WEB

The Web is the first high-impact digital convergence technology, and it has single-handedly moved the entire thrust of digital convergence forward. Why? Here are three important reasons:

(1) The Web has incredible appeal. This fact has stimulated a vision of a new world of innovation based on the technologies of digital convergence. Consumers, technology providers, media companies, communications providers, and entrepreneurs all share this vision.

(2) The Web has become a universal user interface. Those seeking to develop new digital technologies, resources, and services can assume that many users have access to the Web via a Web browser. Thus, the Web browser represents a huge marketplace and a solid platform from which these newly developed digital technologies will be launched.

(3) The Web has stimulated a huge surge in the use of the Internet. The Internet has been around for many years, but the introduction of the Web has created a huge demand for access, resulting in aggressive growth in the scope and capability of this critical infrastructure.

WHAT IS THE WORLD WIDE WEB?

The World Wide Web refers to the global accumulation of all Internet-accessible Web pages and content. In its most basic form, the Web is a system for accessing hyperlinked pages of textual information that are located throughout the Internet (the global system of interconnected networks described in Chapter 5). Web pages are created by using HTML (Hypertext Markup Language), and each Web page contains textual content and special markup tags that specify formatting and other characteristics of the HTML document.

HTML Code	Your Web Browser Displays
You can <I>italicize</I> and <B>bold</B> some text	You can *italicize* and **bold** some text
You can <A HREF="welcome.html">link</A> to another Web page	You can link to another Web page
You can <A HREF="http://www.ibm.com">link</A> to an external Web site	You can link to an external Web site

When you wish to view a particular HTML document, your browser software instructs a Web server to locate that document by using its Web address, or URL (uniform resource locator). The URL will look something like this: *http://www.som.syr.edu/video/index.htm*. The server sends the requested page back to your computer, and it is then displayed by your browser, using the formatting tags and text present in the HTML file. When highlighted text links are clicked, they provide immediate access to other Web pages that have more information and/or additional links. A linked page can be located on the same Web server or on another Internet-accessible Web server anywhere else on the planet.

WEB EXTENSIONS

Add a bevy of extensions to the original notion of the Web described above, and you have today's interactive, media-rich World Wide Web.

One of the most prominent extensions is the inclusion of graphics. These graphics are usually JPEG or GIF images, and an HTML tag specifies the location of these image files on the Web server. The server transmits the images to the browser, and they are included with the rest of the page display.

The Web can also provide access to digital resources that require software external to the browser. MS Office documents, proprietary video formats, and many other specialized digital resources can be linked in an HTML page. In some cases, this is fairly simple. A file is loaded on the Web server, and the Web browser simply downloads and saves the resource to a local disk, where the user accesses it with the appropriate application software.

In other cases, a helper application is configured in the browser. When a linked file of a particular type is encountered, the file is downloaded and automatically opened by the helper application. For example, Microsoft Word can be configured as a helper application. If you click on a link to an MS Word file, that file is automatically downloaded and opened by MS Word.

For some Web-accessible content, browser add-in software must be installed in order to interact directly with the digital resource within the browser. Netscape Navigator accomplishes this task with special programs, called plug-ins. Microsoft Internet Explorer uses Active-X controls, an alternative mechanism based on technology developed by Microsoft for its Windows operating systems.

Web page developers can segment the Web browser window into separate, distinct sub-windows, called frames.

The content of each frame can be updated independently. If the content of a particular frame doesn't fit within the confines of that frame, the Web page author will add scroll bars.

Users can also interact with Web pages through electronic forms. These forms come in many styles: fill in the blanks, check boxes, radio buttons, drop-down menus, and so on.

The information collected by Web forms is processed by the Web server via CGI (common gateway interface) programs. A CGI can access databases to perform searches and return values to the user's Web page; calculate values and return the results; automatically generate and send email messages; and interact with a variety of other server-based programs. Because CGIs enable many of the interactions and transactions that drive electronic commerce, such as searching a product database or processing a credit card order, they are very important.

Java is a computer programming environment that is used to create programs to download and execute within the browser. These programs can run on any hardware that has a Java-compatible browser (that is, any computer with Netscape Navigator or MS Internet Explorer). Java greatly extends the programmability of the browser environment. However, large Java programs download slowly, and program execution is often sluggish, especially when compared to programs written and compiled specifically for your hardware and operating system.

In the version 4 releases of both Netscape Navigator and MS Internet Explorer, slightly differing versions of Dynamic HTML were implemented, offering a suite of capabilities that includes:

■A programmable Web-browser scripting language, called Javascript. Although developed by

Netscape, Javascript is supported by browsers from both Netscape and Microsoft. Javascript is similar to Java, but it is much easier to learn and to use; it is also more limited than Java. Because it is still a fairly complex language, however, nonprogrammers will find Javascript challenging.

■Dynamic pages, or cascading style sheets, that allow a Web page designer to include extra information and graphics on pages that are not seen when the Web page is first viewed. The user can access this additional content without initiating another download from the Web server.

Taken together, these extensions build on the original notion of the hypertext World Wide Web. The result is an innovative environment that facilitates new human interactions and new modes of information access and sharing.

CREATING A WEB SITE

When the Web came on the scene just a few years ago, you had to learn the HTML language to create Web pages. Since that time, a multitude of Web page creation tools have been developed that preclude the need for HTML expertise.

For example:

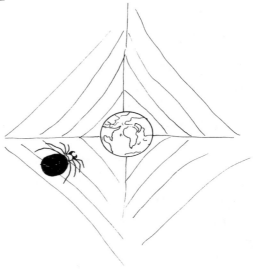

■In Microsoft Word, you have the option of saving your document directly in HTML format. This is one of the simplest and easiest ways to create Web pages. Unfortunately, the formatting options within HTML are much more limited than what is found in MS Word. This often creates confusion and frustration among users who are unaware of the differences.

■Netscape Composer, part of Netscape Communicator, is an easy-to-use HTML editor. This is what we use to teach students and faculty at the School of Management to create basic Web pages.

■Microsoft FrontPage is another popular package for creating Web pages that is easy to learn and use. It has some features that go beyond Composer and MS Office, such as the ability to create pages with frames. Special extensions are also included that make it easy to tap into features of Microsoft's Web server (Internet Information Server), such as Web-based discussion forums.

These tools are suitable for creating a basic Web site, but a variety of more advanced Web page development and Web site management tools exist for those who want to go beyond the basics.

Drumbeat 2000 is a Web site creation tool that allows you to incorporate database functions into your Web pages; NetObjects Fusion is similar to FrontPage, but it gives you more precise control over the graphics on your Web pages; and Linkbot will scan your Web site to look for more than fifty potential problems (broken links, etc.) and then generate a detailed report of those problems.

There are also a number of specialized tools for creating Web multimedia content. They include Macromedia Flash, a powerful tool for creating sophisticated Web animations, and Adobe ImageReady, which quickly identifies the best image format for Web graphics. Adobe ImageReady also enables you to easily create animated GIFs and image maps (clickable images) that serve as Web hyperlinks.

To create your Web site, you need a Web server to run it on. If you are in a large organization that has an enterprise Internet connection, there may be a central Web server (probably based on a Unix server) or a departmental Web server (probably based on a Windows NT, Linux, or Netware server) that you can use for your Web site. Or you may opt to set up your own Web server. Simply run the free Web server built into the operating system of your desktop PC, and get a name for that machine from your network administrator. Of course, some corporations prohibit employees from creating Web sites or restrict Web publishing to the intranet.

For personal Web sites or simple small-business Web sites, there are a number of inexpensive options. Many Internet service providers (ISPs) offer a standard account via dial-up modem that includes access to a Web server and modest storage space for personal Web pages. A number of virtual Web communities, such as GeoCities, Dencity.com, and Tripod, offer free Web services in case your ISP doesn't provide space on one of its Web servers.

If you are an entrepreneur or small business owner, you may want to implement a more sophisticated Web site. To set up a site from scratch, you'll need a Web server, Web server software, and a high-speed Internet connection. Although this is feasible for many people, it can be fairly expensive, time-consuming, and technically challenging. There are outsourcing options you may want to consider.

Web hosting. Web hosting companies and many Internet service providers offer Web hosting. This usually includes a set of services and facilities on their Internet-connected Web server that you secure with a setup fee and an ongoing monthly fee. Web hosting services and facilities can include:

- a storage space for your Web site on a Web server;
- a name for your Web site, such as *www.digital-convergence.com*;
- processing, inventory management, and reporting facilities for e-commerce transactions; and
- Web server extensions (such as CGIs) and access to a database management system.

You may opt to choose an ISP or Web hosting service that will let you maintain your Web server at its location and on its network. This is appropriate if you expect to attract heavy traffic, require total control of your Web server, or need special Web server software that most ISPs won't support.

Web site development and management. You can hire a Web developer or a Web development team to manage your site and create your Web content and services. This can be as

— WEB Developer

— Computer Programmer

— MultiMedia WHIZ

simple as hiring a high school computer nerd for peanuts. Or it can be an expensive contract with a large Web services consulting company that has a highly paid staff of Web developers, computer programmers, and multimedia professionals.

E-commerce functions. Creating a basic Web site is straightforward, and most people can figure out how to put up a simple product catalog. But the back-end processing required for an e-commerce product catalog is not trivial. If you want to sell products, you may choose to outsource this aspect of your site. There are several companies that offer e-commerce services to businesses.

The whole enchilada. You may want to find an individual consultant, a Web development firm, Web hosting service, or an ISP that will take care of your entire site—Web server, Web development, and e-commerce services. This is attractive if there is no expertise within your organization to create and operate a Web site. You should keep in mind, however, that you will end up with less control over your site. Also, it is difficult for a paid consultant to gain the intimate understanding of your business that is necessary to maximize the positive impact of your Web presence.

INTERNET STREAMING MEDIA

Streaming media has come a long way in the past few years, and it is one of the digital convergence technologies that I am most keen on. Like the Web, it enables individuals, entrepreneurs, and corporate workgroups to creatively deploy simple and inexpensive off-the-shelf technology to reach out to people globally.

How It Works

A brief description of Real Networks' streaming media implementation will give you a general idea of how streaming media technology works.

(1) Using proprietary compression technology, Real Networks' encoder compresses digital content, which is typically in WAV or AVI format. The resulting digital file is stored on

the Internet server (Unix or Windows NT) that is running the Real Server software.

(2) Access to the digital audio and video content is initiated through a Web page link that kicks off a client server interaction between the Real Server and the Real Player. The Real Player is client software that must be installed prior to accessing any Real Media. It is configured as a helper application. The Web link includes the address of the Real Server.

(3) The Real Server transmits the audio or video file to the Real Player in a steady, uninterrupted stream. The stream is transported via User Datagram Protocol (UDP), which is described in Chapter 5. The Real Server has a limited number of concurrent streams per license agreement. For example, the free server I run is limited to 25 concurrent streams. If the server is already over its quota, the stream request is rejected.

(4) The Real Player stores several seconds of incoming audio or video in a buffer (a temporary media staging area on the PC hard disk) and then begins to play that audio or video from the buffer. This buffering enables a steady display even though stream transmission may see bursts and delays.

(5) Additional interactions between server and client monitor the flow of the stream. Adjustments can be made to deal with network disruptions (throttling back data transmission if congestion is detected) or user requests (pausing the stream when the user clicks Real Player's "Pause" button).

The Real Networks implementation is standard among streaming media vendors. Alternate compression and multimedia integration schemes, increased scalability, or support for high-quality media (such as MPEG-1 or MP3) are features found in competing products. Real Networks and Microsoft have been the leading developers and vendors of streaming media technology, but Apple Computer is now challenging these two with a new version of Quicktime that supports streaming.

The buffered playback used in streaming media is amazingly effective for counteracting network congestion and delay. Delays can effectively disable a real-time interactive application (such as videoconferencing or Internet telephony), but the buffering technique in streaming media actually introduces delay, thereby masking the variable delay of the network. Because this works so well, I'm very upbeat about the immediate future of streaming media.

ON DEMAND VS. "LIVE BROADCAST" AND UNICAST VS. MULTICAST

One way of delivering streaming media is from a compressed media file stored on a media server. This enables on-demand access for anyone who wants to view the media, whenever they want to view it. There is a great deal of media content on the Internet that is available on demand.

The alternative is to deliver a "live" stream, similar to a television or radio broadcast, where the user must access the stream while it's being "broadcast" or "cybercast." Many radio stations and some television stations encode their programming to provide a continual cybercast. Live feeds are also common for events such as technology conference keynote speeches. Occasionally a mainstream event, such as the Clinton impeachment hearing, is broadcast live on the Net. Broadcast.com (*http://www.broadcast.com*) is the most well-known portal for accessing live and on-demand streaming media.

Sometimes events are broadcast as live events when there appears to be no compelling reason to do so. For example, a Victoria's Secret fashion show drew millions of prospective viewers. Unfortunately, most were unable to see the show. Why? Streaming media does not yet scale effectively to serve millions of simultaneous users.

Unicast streaming delivers a separate stream to each and every user. Considerable bandwidth and server resources are consumed by unicast streaming when an audio or video source gets lots of hits. Thus, it takes significant server and network resources to serve even thousands of simultaneous users. You can begin to see why a very popular cybercast, such as the Victoria's Secret fashion show, did not scale to meet demand.

A pseudo-broadcast mode, called multicasting, is an alternative to unicast. Multicasting carries a single stream through multicast-enabled routers to those users who have subscribed to the stream.

Multicasting can serve many more users than unicast transmission due to its efficient use of bandwidth and servers.

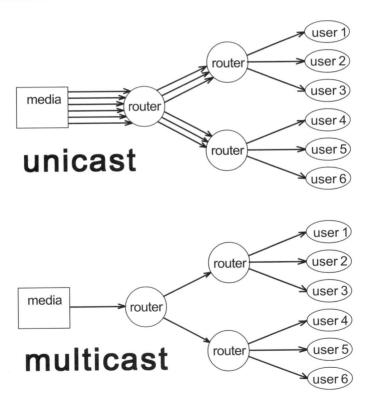

Unfortunately, multicast eliminates the on-demand option, because all users receive the single stream at the same time.

Multicast streaming also requires that network routers be multicast enabled, but that is not yet the case for all Internet routers. At this point, multicasting is only feasible on a corporate intranet or an Internet segment under control of a single Internet service provider, where the network administrators within the corporate IT group, or ISP, can ensure that all routers are multicast enabled. UUNet is one of the first ISPs to support multicasting throughout its network infrastructure.

Some streaming media vendors support stream propagation as an alternative to multicasting. This technique delivers a unicast stream to multiple dispersed media servers, each dedicated to serving a unique segment of the Internet. It spreads the load among multiple servers, and it moves bandwidth utilization closer to the users, obviating the need for duplicate unicast transmissions across many network segments. In this way, unicast transmissions are able to scale up for a larger numbers of users.

I still can't understand why Victoria's Secret didn't offer the fashion show in on-demand mode. They could have attracted many more users, over time, than they could ever serve in a single live cybercast. Of course, they did receive considerable coverage in the news media. Maybe that was part of the motivation.

As digital convergence gains momentum and provides us with new opportunities, our challenge is to think creatively about how we want to use this new technology. That means exploring new modes of human communication and interaction rather than moving traditional television, telephone, and radio to the Internet.

The power of streaming media is not in its ability to broadcast live media to millions of viewers or listeners. We have TV and radio for that. Its power lies largely in its ability to narrow-cast, thus connecting individuals, entrepreneurs, and corporate workgroups who are creatively reaching out to customers, colleagues, business partners, friends, and family.

VIDEOCONFERENCING

For many years, videoconferencing technology was used almost exclusively in expensive, high-end corporate and educational settings. Studios, high-tech classrooms, and electronic boardrooms were constructed and outfitted with high-quality equipment at great cost.

Three relatively recent developments have led to much more widespread adoption of this technology: First, videoconferencing has gone digital. Accordingly, the cost of the equipment for videoconferencing equipment has decreased dramatically. A high-quality system for small group conferencing is available for around $10,000. A desktop videoconferencing unit for business-quality videoconferencing will cost around $2,500, including the cost of the PC. Low-end Internet videoconferencing systems can be configured for under $200, using an existing computer. Videoconferencing technology is clearly within the financial grasp of the individual, the entrepreneur, the workgroup, and the small firm.

Second, videoconferencing connectivity is readily available. The global digital network infrastructure, including the Internet and the global ISDN network, enables ubiquitous access to videoconferencing connectivity in countries that have progressive, technology-based economies. This includes the U.S., Europe, Japan, and many other areas worldwide.

Third, standards are now in place. Not long ago, digital videoconferencing systems were strictly proprietary. You could only conference with systems from the same manufacturer. Now vendors offer videoconferencing technology that adheres to new International Telecommunications Union standards, allowing systems from different vendors to be used together.

The ITU has coordinated the following videoconferencing standards suites:

- H.320—videoconferencing over ISDN lines;
- H.323—videoconferencing over packet-switched networks; and
- T.120—data and application sharing.

Each of these umbrella standards include several other standards for video compression, audio compression, conference setup, signaling, security, and so forth. H.320 was the first videoconference standards suite, and it had an immediate impact on ISDN-based videoconferencing equipment and usage. Now, H.323 and T.120 are beginning to have the same effect on intranet and Internet videoconferencing.

To give you a feel for the capabilities of different types of videoconferencing systems, we'll profile three separate systems—one rollout system and two desktop systems.

PictureTel is a prominent name in videoconferencing, and this company has been a market leader for some time. A typical rollout system from PictureTel is capable of more than 20 frames per second, videoconferencing over three ISDN lines at 384 Kbps (3 times 128 Kbps).

The Syracuse University School of Management owns a PictureTel rollout system that consists of a 32-inch Sony monitor, a Bose speaker system, and an omnidirectional microphone unit that will easily pick up audio from any part of a small- to medium-sized room. All this is bundled on a mobile cart. The system is based on an IBM-compatible computer, is H.320 compatible, and includes technology that provides full

duplex audio without feedback or echo. The video is some-what fuzzy when there is lots of motion or panning, but it is fine for talking-head videoconferences.

This system cost us around $30,000 a couple of years ago. At a presentation I recently attended, I saw a very similar system from another vendor—for only $10,000!

The PictureTel rollabout systems are great for small con-ferences, and they work well for some larger groups, too. We use ours regularly for a U.S. Army executive education pro-gram. A Pentagon official will make a presentation, then en-gage in a Q&A session with thirty or so Army civilian executives.

Intel ProShare is a desktop system that can be used to videoconference through the ISDN network or across the Internet (or a corporate intranet). The ProShare package fea-tures an ISDN adapter (called an NT-1) and a dedicated cir-cuit board that must be installed on your computer for video capture and ISDN communication. Included is a small cam-era that you attach to the top of your computer monitor and an earpiece that has a built-in microphone. Also included is an input for a second video source, such as a VCR. The sys-tem is H.320 and H.323 compatible.

ProShare is capable of video at 15 frames per second over a single ISDN line at 128 Kbps. This is far less than the PictureTel unit, but it is still quite acceptable for most people. A conference across a corporate intranet can achieve higher frame rates, provided there is plenty of network band-width.

I've used our ProShare system to conference with a class of about a hundred students in our auditorium. I just connect the desktop PC to one of our ceiling-mounted video projec-tors and the room's speaker system, plug into the ISDN line, use a single handheld shotgun microphone (which helps to minimize echo)—and I'm in business. Although I have to serve as moderator and relay student questions to the remote speaker, it works just fine. Based on the feedback I've received, students seem to like it, too.

One of the great things about the ProShare system is that it enables application and data sharing. When you conference with another ProShare user, you can open and share documents and applications. How often have you discussed a document, presentation, or spreadsheet or talked about a software program over the phone? ProShare videoconferencing allows you to see and hear the person you are speaking with, view and manipulate any documents, or fire up that software you're discussing. ProShare is an excellent collaboration tool.

ProShare's data and application-sharing capability was implemented through a partnership with Microsoft. It is based on software developed by Microsoft for NetMeeting, another Internet videoconferencing program. The NetMeeting data and application-sharing capability adheres to the ITU T.120 standard. In addition to application sharing, you can also share a whiteboard, transfer a file, and type messages to your conference partners in chat mode.

CU-SeeMe Pro is a low-end Internet/intranet desktop videoconferencing solution that was originally developed at Cornell University, but is now commercially available from White Pine, Inc. This is software-only technology that is similar to (and competes with) Microsoft's NetMeeting. To videoconference with CU-SeeMe, you must install a compatible video-capture setup on your own. Many users buy an inexpensive video camera and connect it directly to the serial port or the USB (universal serial bus) of a new PC.

CU-SeeMe is a low-end videoconferencing package, and the quality of the video and audio is marginal. However, the whole package (including the camera) can be bought for well under $200.

CU-SeeMe operates over the Internet using H.323

technology. An enhanced version of CU-SeeMe, called CU-SeeMe Pro, also includes T.120-compatible data and application sharing. As with ProShare, CU-SeeMe incorporates Microsoft's NetMeeting technology.

CU-SeeMe was originally developed in conjunction with a reflector, which is a server that reflects all the video streams it receives back to all participants. White Pine now offers a reflector-like server, called an MCS (multipoint conference server). Unlike a CU-SeeMe reflector, however, the White Pine MCS is H.323 compatible. Several H.323-compatible clients can meet at a CU-SeeMe MCS, and each can see and hear everyone else. This application has great potential for training, distance learning, and other group interactions. The Cornell CU-SeeMe reflector is free, but the White Pine MCS costs several thousand dollars, not including the hardware.

H.320 ISDN multipoint conference servers are also available, and these MCSs are often referred to as bridges. ISDN videoconferencing users may opt to outsource this function to a telecommunications company, such as Sprint, or a company whose primary business is bridging ISDN multipoint calls, such as Connexus, InView, or 1-800-Video-On.

INTERNET TELEPHONY

Internet telephony is a strategically important digital convergence technology because:

■The first implementations will be audio only, so bandwidth constraints do not constitute an insurmountable barrier to widespread deployment. However, congestion and latency may still be nagging problems.

■As this rich-media technology is widely implemented, it will pave the way for a host of other digital convergence technologies and applications.

In this way, we will move closer to a full-blown digital convergence architecture that will serve all corporate and consumer voice, data, and video needs.

■ Due to its great commercial potential, Internet telephony is being pursued by the heavy hitters in the telecommunications and networking industry, including AT&T, Lucent, Cisco, and Nortel.

Internet telephony started out as a fairly simple application. Two Internet-connected computers—equipped with an Internet phone software program (Internet Phone or WebPhone), a sound card, and a microphone—could connect to each other and carry on an audio conference. When it worked well, it was somewhat like making free long-distance calls. You just had to have an Internet connection. For most consumers, this was a local modem call to an Internet service provider; corporate networks provided an always-on Internet connection. The Internet would then carry the long-distance voice-data streams.

Early Internet phone technology was inferior to conventional phone service. The lack of Internet quality of service made this a hit-or-miss proposition, and users experienced

garbled or choppy audio when Internet congestion caused data packet loss. Many early Internet phone products were also half-duplex, allowing only one participant to speak at any given moment. This service resembled a walkie-talkie more than a telephone.

The Internet still lacks the QoS required for reliable point-to-point Internet phone calls, but Internet telephony is no longer just a couple of PCs talking across the Internet. Internet telephony technology has grown in scope to include:

♦ Internet fax technologies and services;

♦ gateways between Internet networks (that is, an intranet or a segment of an ISP network) and traditional public switched phone networks;

♦ ethernet-based Internet phones (they look the same as your home or office phone);

♦ one-click access to a corporate call center from a user's Web browser; and

♦ ISP-based Internet telephony services.

Internet telephony derives its benefits from a combination of facts and circumstances:

■Packet networks, such as the Internet, make more efficient use of bandwidth than circuit-switched networks, such as the phone network.

■Internet telephony enables corporations to consolidate voice and data services over a single packet-switched network infrastructure.

■In the U.S., federal regulations add a few cents to each long-distance phone call to subsidize phone service in rural areas. Internet telephone calls are exempt from these fees.

■Because this technology is digital, Internet telephony can be easily extended with additional services. For example, Internet telephony can be integrated with Web information and transactions, and it can be extended with digital video.

Internet telephony is showing the signs of a technology that will dramatically change a whole segment of the communications industry in the near future. In the process, other rich-media communication technologies and applications are also gaining momentum. This is exciting, but you should remember that Internet telephony is still immature. Use caution when deploying Internet telephony technologies and services.

MESSAGE-BASED COMMUNICATION

EMAIL

Internet telephony and videoconferencing overcome distance barriers to offer real-time, rich-media communication. This is referred to as synchronous communication. Email (electronic mail) is a communication mechanism that is very different.

- Email eliminates the barriers of distance as well as time. When you post a message, the recipients will see it, but not necessarily the moment you send it. This is known as asynchronous communication.
- Email relies primarily on message-oriented, text-based communication. This is the lowest-common-denominator communications medium that ensures nearly universal access.
- Network constraints may introduce annoying delays, but network anomalies cannot diminish the quality and integrity of an email communication.

To communicate via Internet email, you compose a text message using a desktop email client program and then click on a "Send" button, or icon, in that program to send it off. Your email client software transfers your message to an outgoing email server. Next, the server initiates an Internet transfer to a receiving email server by use of SMTP (Simple Mail Transfer Protocol). To receive your email message, the recipient is most likely to use one of the following mechanisms.

Web-based Mail. Email services (such as those available from Yahoo! and Hotmail) offer a popular option for reading email. Using your Web browser, you go to the Web site where you can access your inbox through a series of log-in forms and Web pages. The beauty of Web email is that you can retrieve your email from any browser anywhere on the Internet.

Web mail is becoming quite common, especially at sites where email is a tool for creating and building community. For example, the Buffalo Sabres hockey team offers Web-based email through its Web site, and I have an account there. You can send me email at *onetimer@sabreshockey.com.* To be honest, though, I don't log in and read my Buffalo Sabres email all that often.

POP Mail. Your email messages are downloaded (or popped) from a personal email inbox located on a POP (Post Office Protocol) mail server. Microsoft Outlook, Netscape Messenger, and Eudora are the POP-compatible email client software packages usually used, and most Internet service providers offer POP mail as the standard email service.

IMAP Mail. Some corporate networks are employing a new Internet email server mechanism that is based on IMAP (Internet Message Access Protocol). Rather than downloading your messages, you can read and manage them on an IMAP server. The email clients mentioned above now support access to IMAP email servers. IMAP is very useful if you read email in multiple locations. When you download (POP) your mail to a specific PC, you disable access to those messages from other PCs. For this reason, IMAP has made life much easier for those who regularly read email on different machines in different locations. At the School of Management, we converted to IMAP email for our students and many of our faculty last year.

Email client software makes it easy to organize your messages in file folders, search message folders, and send messages to multiple recipients. Email clients also enable users to send and receive file attachments, whether documents, spreadsheets, programs, Web pages, or any other computer file. This is a very important email enhancement that I, like millions of others, use on a daily basis to share information with colleagues and customers.

Unfortunately, email attachments can often cause problems when email clients from different vendors are involved in transmission and receipt. At the School of Management, we use attachments extensively in our distance learning program, and I spend lots of time fiddling with attachments that our email software can't recognize or decode automatically.

Email discussion servers (also called listservs) enable groups of people to interact easily by distributing messages posted on the discussion server to everyone who has "subscribed" to the listserv. A listserv is a great way for people who share an interest or special need to maintain a dialog and exchange information. Listservs are used extensively at the School of Management to facilitate class discussions outside of the classroom, disseminate information to faculty and staff, and keep in touch with alumni.

Email is extremely convenient and reliable. Though text-based electronic mail lacks the impressiveness of many rich-media digital convergence technologies, its ability to ensure timely, efficient communication between individuals and among groups makes it an invaluable tool.

GROUPWARE

Email is a simple, straightforward message-based communication tool. Groupware technology takes message-oriented communication one step further. In a groupware system, text messages are the core mechanism for a more comprehensive communications environment that integrates discussion forums, group scheduling, information sharing, group voting, work flow, and electronic mail.

Some of the most popular groupware technologies, such as Lotus Notes and Novell Groupwise, were originally developed to run over proprietary network protocols for use in isolated corporate networks. They have been updated to run over the TCP/IP protocols, so this powerful collaboration technology can now be deployed across an intranet, extranet, or the Internet. In a complex corporate environment, message-based groupware tools can facilitate effective and efficient communication within a corporate task force, workgroup, or across the entire enterprise.

CHAT

Like videoconferencing and Internet telephony, chat is a text-based communication tool that enables synchronous communication. Your messages are posted to a real-time electronic bulletin board so that the participants of the chat session can see them in real time. You can see what everyone else posts as well. An ongoing chat session, where people are able to join and leave, is called a chat room.

Because chat is a text-only tool, it is minimally affected by Internet bandwidth constraints and bottlenecks. Occasionally, however, network problems introduce an annoying delay between the time a chat participant posts a message and the time it is seen by the other chat participants.

Chat is a long-standing digital convergence application

technology that really caught on several years ago. Like email, it is a rock-solid technology that is universally accessible. Chat is extremely popular for personal entertainment, and millions of people chat in Internet and America Online (AOL) chat rooms every day.

Chat has some potential as a useful technology for distance learning and for some business applications. It provides a crude form of real-time communication, and you can set up private chat rooms if you want to minimize distractions or eliminate eavesdroppers. At the School of Management, we set up a discussion forum server that includes a chat function, but we use it infrequently. It just doesn't generate much interest among our faculty, students, or alumni.

PUSH TECHNOLOGY

Typical push technology consists of an Internet client/server system that continually refreshes your desktop with news and information. You don't have to lift a finger to get these continuous updates. From your point of view, the system "pushes" data to your computer. In most cases, however, the client program on your PC actually pulls data from the Internet server.

I'll bet only a few of you use push technology. A couple of years ago, the trade media was predicting the demise of the Web browser in favor of push technology. Push technology was overly publicized by the high-tech industry and the trade media, but it has never lived up to its hype. Thus, push technology offers a good reminder to be cautious before embracing the Next Big Thing.

Pointcast was the first push technology to gain a wide audience. As a subscriber, you complete an electronic profile that specifies categories of information you are interested in. The client program periodically polls an Internet server and downloads any new information pertinent to the categories you've chosen. You can then peruse the information that is delivered. Pointcast can provide continuous updates of news, stock prices, weather forecasts, horoscopes, and a host of other information resources. This software also doubles as a screen saver. In screen-saver mode, it continually refreshes your screen with incoming news and information.

When Pointcast first came on the scene, it was a bit of a novelty. It had great content, and it met with immediate success. Only a matter of months passed before there were dozens of new push technology vendors, each with its own proprietary spin on pushing news and information across the Internet.

Eventually, even Netscape and Microsoft built push technology into their browsers. These include:

- Netscape's Netcaster, based on Dynamic HTML;
- Internet Explorer's Subscriptions feature; and
- Microsoft's Channel Definition Format, an XML-based specification for creating Web-based push "channels."

The problem with push technology is that it is a technical solution to a nonproblem, and it doesn't add significant value to the Internet experience.

Push technology eliminates human intervention and the network transmission delay inherent in Web access, but most people aren't all that annoyed by that intervention and delay. If I want current news and information, I can pull up any number of Internet news services in a matter of seconds. In fact, I have a news site set up as my default home page, so I just click the "Home" button to get the latest news and information. The Web provides a flexible exploratory information-access model that most people really appreciate even if they sometimes find it tedious, confusing, or time-consuming.

The luster has worn off push technology. Many push technology vendors have either been gobbled up by larger software development firms, or they have refocused their product for some niche application. Such applications include the real-time push of pricing information in the financial services sector or pushing software updates to client machines, thus freeing the user from downloading and applying fixes and updates. Pointcast has seen its subscriber base decline, and it was recently purchased by Idealab Inc., a venture capital company that reportedly plans to turn Pointcast into an e-commerce service.

The Web phenomenon was, and is, special. It will be some time before any huge change occurs in the way users access Internet information resources.

DIGITAL TELEVISION

Digital television is slowly becoming a reality, and the meandering course of its evolution tells us much about the evolution of digital convergence.

High definition TV (HDTV) offers a significant increase in picture quality and sound over conventional television, and delivering that quality was at one time the primary goal of digital television. As the trend toward digital convergence has accelerated, the objectives have broadened to include an emphasis on interactive television. It is now clear that digital television will become another Internet access mechanism.

Long before digital HDTV signals were first broadcast on a regular basis in a handful of major U.S. cities, Web-based interactive television had already been launched.

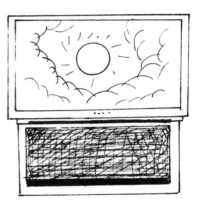

Here's how it works. The vertical blanking interval is the brief period when television picture scanning moves from the bottom of the screen back to the top. It is used to send closed-captioned information. Intel's Intercast technology utilized the vertical blanking interval of the conventional analog television signal to send Web pages that could be decoded and displayed on a properly equipped computer.

Web-TV Plus and Web-TV for Windows have integrated and extended Intercast technology to promote more widespread adoption of interactive television. Several broadcasters, including the Sci-Fi Network, MSNBC, The Weather Channel, and Turner Classic Movies, have all offered enhanced Web-TV content.

Various industry consortiums, such as the Intel-led Advanced Television Engineering Forum (ATVEF), are developing standards for creating digital content and services that can be delivered in conjunction with a fully digital television broadcast. These standards are based largely on HTML.

As high-definition digital television standards were being developed and proposed to the Federal Communications Commission, picture format became an issue. It brought to the fore two competing visions of digital television: one focused on high-definition picture quality; the other emphasizing digital interactive television.

You'll recall from Chapter 2 that a television uses an electron beam to scan the inside of the picture tube and energize red, blue, and green picture elements. Every other line of the video image is scanned in one sweep of the screen, thus taking two sweeps of the electron beam to create the picture you see. This is called interlace scanning. Progressive scan, an alternative scanning mechanism, scans every line in a single sweep of the tube. This is the scan format that is used in computer monitors.

Progressive scanning reduces flicker around text and other fine-edged video elements. Interlaced scanning is thought by many to produce a higher-quality picture for high-motion video (such as sports), but I haven't yet had the opportunity to do a side-by-side comparison.

The formats being proposed for the new digital television standard were identified with the number of scan lines followed by an "I" or a "P", indicating interlaced or progressive scanning. Therefore, 720P indicates a progressive scan format with 720 lines of resolution. The set of formats under consideration included a progressive scan format roughly equivalent to today's television quality (420P) on up to a very high-resolution interlaced format (1080I) that is considered high-end HDTV.

So how did some of the major players line up behind these formats?

■Most broadcasters wanted to emphasize the improved quality of HDTV over conventional television. They favored the ultrahigh-resolution 1080I format.

■Computer companies wanted to emphasize interactive, Internet-based digital television. They favored lower-resolution, progressive scan formats, such as 480P and 720P, that are compatible with today's computer technology.

■Because many cable companies are now providing Internet access services, they were also supportive of the lower-resolution, progressive scan formats. Computer-friendly formats will fuel their Internet access business, an increasing source of revenue for today's cable companies. Cable companies also have limited bandwidth in their cable infrastructures, so the lower-resolution formats are favored because they are less bandwidth intensive. The same bandwidth needed to carry a single 1080I HDTV program can carry multiple digital programs using the lower-resolution formats.

In the end, the FCC decided to let the marketplace determine digital television picture formats. There are now well over a dozen formats in the running. We'll just have to wait and see how the market shapes the deployment and adoption of these formats.

For most of us, digital television is still a couple of years away from becoming a reality, but its evolution is being profoundly affected by the digital convergence phenomenon. Stay tuned to see how this remarkable transition flows from a good idea with a hotly debated future to home and office use. How do you think you will first engage high-definition interactive digital television? The choice might be:

- ◆ with an expensive HDTV set, probably at an electronics boutique or upscale department store (unless you have plenty of disposable income to take it home with you);
- ◆ with a set-top box that converts the digital broadcast (received through your cable, satellite dish, or rooftop antenna) to a format compatible with your analog TV; or
- ◆ with the purchase of an inexpensive add-in card for your PC, which you'll be able to configure for HDTV reception.

Up until this point, the focus of this book has been technology, and we've covered a lot of ground. This is useful information, but you're probably anxious to start thinking seriously about how *you* might use new digital convergence technologies. In the final chapter, we'll explore the ins and outs of putting digital convergence technology to work—for you.

8

SELECT AND IMPLEMENT

The digital convergence phenomenon will create many opportunities for you to move your business, career, and personal agenda forward. Let's take a look at some of the key issues and strategies that will make or break your efforts to successfully deploy these new technologies.

New, rapidly evolving digital convergence technologies and applications continually present a wide range of possibilities for furthering individual or organizational goals and objectives. Examples include providing better customer service; reaching new markets; extending and strengthening your network of business partners; promoting your image and your message; and improving your ability to collaborate and interact with business partners, friends, or family.

Successful employment of any new technology results from a process that (1) matches needs and opportunities with available technologies, and (2) implements the selected technologies according to the context in which they will be used.

This may be as simple as securing the services of an international Internet telephony provider to save money on international calls, or as complex as implementing a corporate extranet for enhanced communication and interaction with business partners.

If you are to take on the challenge of pursuing new technology, you will need to do the following:

- ♦ develop a game plan to continually learn about new technology;
- ♦ research specific technologies and learn how these technologies are evolving;
- ♦ match needs and opportunities with emerging technologies and available products; and
- ♦ develop an implementation strategy that will work in your organization (whether self-run, part-time enterprise, or giant global corporation)

Let's examine these aspects of implementing technology in greater detail.

COMMIT TO CONTINUOUS LEARNING

In this section I will introduce learning resources and methods (taken from my own experience) that can help to equip you with the knowledge you need to move forward. The ideas presented can be built upon as you work to establish your own learning style, but they are by no means exhaustive. You must develop a game plan for learning that is both efficient and effective for you.

This book has offered a broad framework for understanding technology evolution, plus a healthy dose of information about specific technologies, thus making it a good starting point. Digital convergence technologies are evolving at a torrid pace, and you must be willing to make a sustained effort to keep up with new technology trends. This is essential if you want to use new technology successfully.

Digital convergence technologies and products are numerous and complex, and no one can know it all. Few people have the time to become expert on even one of these technologies. The trick, then, is to get very good at learning a subset of all there is to know and to make sure that subset is really useful to you.

Because there is no clear formula for how to accomplish this goal effectively, you will learn by trial and error. The most important thing is to recognize that you are after a useful subset. This approach will offer some psychological relief when dealing with the enormous volume of rapidly changing information about technology.

You will want to pursue two parallel, but mutually reinforcing, learning efforts. One effort will be to build a broad foundation of technical knowledge. The other is to drill down into the details of a specific technology that may be promising in your particular situation. These two efforts will afford you a knowledge of technologies that are relevant here and now. In addition, you will keep up with technological developments that drive the evolution of new technologies, and you will ensure your ability to spot up-and-coming technologies that may be relevant to your interests, needs, and opportunities.

A number of resources and learning activities can be mixed and matched to suit your learning style and objectives. Here is a brief summary of a few common resources and activities that you will surely want to consider.

Books are an excellent resource that cover all aspects of technology. Comprehensive coverage of many important topics can be found, from analyses of the socioeconomic impact of new technology to nuts-and-bolts information on specific versions of software applications. The book format is great for learning on the go as well as for concentrated study. Some books will serve as priceless references. Others will be throwaways, providing you only with information on a specific technology that may have little staying power.

Because technology evolves at such a rapid pace and because the publishing cycle can be rather lengthy, books may be quickly outdated. This is often a problem with books that focus on a particular version of a particular software package. As soon as a major new version of the software hits the market, these books lose their value. However, in-depth technology books (even those that are slightly out of date) will comprise an excellent resource for building the foundation of understanding needed to skillfully leverage emerging digital convergence technologies.

I recommend that you fire up your Web browser and head for Amazon.com (*http://www.amazon.com*) and BarnesandNoble.com (*http://www.barnesandnoble.com*). Or find a good bookstore and check out the technology section. Get a feel for what is available, and discover what style of book fits you and your learning objectives. Also, check out the online reader reviews via your Web browser, or thumb through a few copies in the bookstore. You'll probably end up buying a book or two. As you read through them, you will quickly build a useful knowledge base.

Trade magazines are another valuable printed resource. Some are news-oriented, while others review the features, capabilities, and limitations of emerging technologies. Like books, magazines have a publishing cycle, but it is relatively short and each issue is dated. By checking the date on the magazine, you can be confident that the information you find is current.

You should consider subscribing to at least a couple of publications. A news weekly will keep you up to date on the broad-brush evolution of new technology. *PC Week*, *Information Week*, or *Inter@ctive Week* are examples of this kind of magazine. A more focused monthly (or semimonthly) magazine or an industry-specific trade magazine will cover technology that is likely to be relevant to your work. Such publications include *PC Magazine*, *New Media*, or *Digital Video Producer*.

Many trade magazines offer free subscriptions. For example, I receive *Inter@ctive Week*, *Internet Week*, *Network Computing*, and *New Media* for free. To qualify, you fill out and return a questionnaire that details your job function and purchasing power. This is a great way to get excellent information and analyses at no cost.

The Web is one of the best resources for learning about technology. The Web offers an enormous collection of useful information on all topics, but it is especially strong when it comes to technology. I always tell people to use technology to learn about technology, and most often that means using the Web.

■Visit a Web information portal (Alta Vista, Lycos, or Yahoo!) to search for information on a particular topic. You can also drill down through

Web content menus to get access to Web resources that relate to your interests and needs.

■Tap into a number of technologically oriented Web resources. C|Net (*http://www.cnet.com*), CMP's Techweb (*http://techweb.cmp.com*), and Ziff Davis's ZDnet (*http://www.zdnet.com*) provide searchable access to current and archival technology articles from a number of online or print-based publications.

■Download white papers on technology topics from vendor Web sites and the Web sites of technology consulting firms.

■Search the Web to locate tutorials and university course materials covering technological topics that interest you. For example, go to Alta Vista at *http://www.altavista.digital.com* and search for "HTML tutorial." You'll find several Web sites that will teach you how to create HTML Web pages.

The Web has become an incredibly rich resource. Compared to trade magazines, books, and vendor manuals, the Web contains a greater variety in the type and quality of information available. The cost of publishing on the Web is low, so anyone can put up a Web site and offer his or her insights. As a result, you'll need to assess the reliability and timeliness of the information you find on the Web.

If you use a well-known, branded information resource, you can be fairly assured of its quality. However, many Web information resources require you to be a little more discerning when determining the reliability and value of the information you find. Fortunately, there are plenty of excellent nonbranded, nontraditional information resources on the Web that will enrich your learning, making it worth the extra time and effort needed to separate the wheat from the chaff.

Learning by doing should be the focus for anyone pursuing new technology. Hands-on activity will help you to understand what makes technology tick and what makes it succeed or fail. Even if you expect to outsource some of the technical aspects of your projects, you should still learn about technology through direct experience.

I've worked with a few professors who have a skewed notion of what technology can do and how it can be realistically used. Because they've avoided technology for many years and have limited personal experience, their perspective has been shaped largely by the media. They don't possess an understanding of the flaws and foibles of these new tools, which is a must if you are to move forward in any serious fashion. Until you experience the rough edges of technology, you are in no position to plan for or implement the newer technologies.

Learning from others is an activity that offers great returns. Interacting with people who are more experienced or are pursuing a technology that interests you can save enormous amounts of time. It can also shed light on easily overlooked issues. Some of these individuals can be found among colleagues and coworkers whom you contact on a regular basis, or you may need to seek out people external to your locale. Usenet news and email listservs are two mechanisms for finding and electronically interacting with knowledgeable individuals who might help you out.

Usenet news is a text-based electronic discussion forum that facilitates discourse on a wide range of topics. Usenet discussions take place on electronic bulletin boards called newsgroups. Many of the newsgroup topics are technical in nature, and some of the most well-versed experts on technical topics monitor these newsgroups and respond to technical questions.

Access to Usenet newsgroup discussions is via a news feed available from your Internet service provider or a Web site, such as Deja News (*http://www.dejanews.com*). How to gain access and use Usenet news feeds is covered in most introductory Internet texts written for novices. Yahoo! and other Web portals can link you to Web resources that describe Usenet news in detail.

There are many technically oriented listservs as well, forming an excellent source of contacts (listservs were introduced in Chapter 7). Several Web sites exist that provide descriptions and subscription information for a variety of useful listservs. L-Soft International maintains a searchable catalog of over 20,000 listservs at *http://www.lsoft.com/catalist.html.*

Instruction is another excellent option for learning about technology, whether one-to-one, face-to-face, or via distance-learning technology. Thousands of seminars, workshops, and video training courses are offered at colleges and universities. In addition, there is a host of digital learning options that range from training materials on CD-ROM, to college-based independent study, to the sort of new wave digital learning that Ziff Davis University offers at around $7.95 per course!

Formal instruction can be especially useful if you are

extremely busy and find it difficult to take time from day-to-day activities to learn through reading and hands-on exploration. Some people also find that instructor-student interactions and student-student interactions reinforce what they have learned from lecture, reading, and practice.

FOLLOW THE EVOLUTION OF PROMISING TECHNOLOGIES

As I pointed out at the beginning of this chapter, successfully deploying new technology requires a process that (1) effectively matches opportunities and needs with the possibilities that new technologies afford, and (2) implements the selected technology within the given constraints of the project or task.

This may sound like a two-step, straight-line process, but it is actually a continual and iterative process. As you are gaining the experience of implementing a selected technology, the needs and opportunities of your organization may change, and new technologies will emerge and evolve. This latter aspect of the process is the subject of this section.

This book offers a high-level view of the digital convergence phenomenon that is driving the evolution of digital technologies. As you dig deeper and begin to focus on the specific technologies that might offer the highest potential payoffs in your unique situation, you must take into account the factors that affect the evolution of specific technologies.

You will be encouraged by this golden rule: The cost of a technology will decline while its performance, functionality, ease of implementation, and ease of use will increase. This one simple notion is responsible for a steady stream of powerful, readily accessible new technologies that are empowering us all.

Although this golden rule is indeed a reality, you won't be surprised to hear that technology evolution is not quite so simple. Some technologies languish for a period of time, usually because they have a significant flaw or they don't offer enough practical utility. After a while, they may move into the mainstream or they may just fade away.

Let's discuss some of the concepts of technology evolution using videoconferencing as a typical example.

Videoconferencing technology has been with us for decades. In fact, a videophone was demonstrated at the 1964 World's Fair, although that particular technology never caught on due to the prohibitively expensive phone lines required.

Like many other digital convergence technologies, videoconferencing has recently experienced a rapid increase in functionality that has been accompanied by an equally rapid decrease in price.

Prior to 1990, videoconferencing was relegated primarily to corporate and distance learning applications, such as executive conferences and training courses. Studios, executive conference rooms, and conference-ready classrooms were set up for videoconferencing via satellite or leased lines. The special equipment required was purchased at considerable cost.

Now, videoconferencing technology is available in a much wider variety of configurations. Low-end digital systems, costing a few hundred dollars, are available for use over standard phone lines or the Internet. High-end videoconferencing systems, costing tens of thousands of dollars, use multiple ISDN lines or leased lines to provide crisp, clear audio and video.

The recent rise in videoconferencing capability, flexibility, and availability represents the typical evolutionary scenario of digital convergence. It is characterized by the elements described below.

Technological breakthroughs. They are a fact of modern life, and they occur at an ever increasing rate. New developments in videoconferencing technology and applications have been propelled by breakthroughs in the processing capacity and media capabilities of the desktop PC as well as advances in digital network technologies. The development of these technologies has accelerated and the mass production of videoconferencing components has become less expensive due to other technological breakthroughs that have affected engineering and manufacturing processes.

Standards. They provide a foundation of functionality that boosts vendor support for, and user interest in, an emerging technology. The videoconferencing standards of the International Telecommunications Union (ITU) allow vendors to offer interoperable technology. Therefore, conferencing is possible among any external organizations or individuals possessing an ITU-compliant system. These standards have dramatically increased the overall utility of this technology.

The exploding market. In today's market, many more players are mobilized to beat the competition to a superior solution. The rapidly expanding base of prospective consumers and corporate users has created fantastic opportunities for anyone who can build a technology that catches on. Thus, traditional technology providers are stimulated to develop new technology, and, at every turn, a slew of entrepreneurs and start-ups are working to beat them to the punch. The result is technology that evolves at an incredible pace.

The Internet. A new ubiquitous infrastructure for videoconferencing is provided by the Internet. Unfortunately, along with several other real-time, rich-media Internet technologies, desktop PC-based Internet videoconferencing is languishing. The Internet doesn't yet have the necessary capacity and end-to-end quality of service that is required to ensure high-quality audio and video in a real-time conference. The technology still has some utility, but for those applications that require uniform high quality, it is just not up to the task. As a result, Internet videoconferencing is used mostly by hobbyists and others (especially those in the adult entertainment industry) who can live with unreliable, low-quality audio and video. Most business users and others who require quality audio and video are likely to implement ISDN-based videoconferencing systems.

TECHNOLOGICAL MATURITY

Maturity is an important factor to consider when evaluating the potential of a technology for successful deployment. The reliability of immature technologies is usually more limited than that of mature technologies, so it makes sense to focus on mature technologies whenever possible.

At times you just need to exercise patience with some immature technologies. You don't want to expend valuable time, effort, and money on a technology that is not ready for prime time. Given the right circumstances, some technologies will mature in a short period of time. The combination of mature underlying technologies and a large potential market is usually required for rapid maturation.

Occasionally, circumstances arise where the value of an immature or languishing technology (such as Internet videoconferencing) outweighs the extra risk. If there is a definite need or opportunity, and the technology can clearly do the job, then being in the vanguard of those who use an immature emerging technology can be an astute strategy. By anticipating an imminent move of that technology into the mainstream, you will get a jump on the competition. As the technology becomes more widely employed, you will be maximizing its benefit while your competitors are still learning the ropes.

Standards

A basis in standards, or a lack of standards, often says something about the relative maturity of a technology. Immature technologies typically include strictly proprietary technology. Standards can serve to legitimize a technology, thereby attracting increased vendor support and user interest. They also provide an interoperable platform of functionality for further technological development.

Interoperability is important, because it means technology from alternative vendors will provide the same functionality. If you acquire technology from one vendor and their technical support or pricing is out of line with the rest of the market, you are free to purchase the technology from another vendor next time around. Interoperability also means more products that can work together. This fact usually translates into a larger base of users.

Once you've chosen a technology to learn, you should work to understand any relevant standards. You also need to assess the overall breadth of standards adoption in the market for that technology, and whether the products you may be considering adhere to those standards. Unfortunately, this is sometimes a tricky business.

■The relevant standards may be de facto standards, underlying proprietary technology that is implemented uniformly in various products.

■Sometimes competing standards confuse users and fragment a market, especially when different vendors become involved in developing and supporting competing standards.

■Specific products are sometimes said to be standards compliant, but they only implement a subset of the standards specification.

■A product may include additional proprietary functionality that reduces its flexibility and interoperability.

You need to be careful when reading vendor literature that discusses standards. Vendors will provide useful background information, but your best information comes from the standards bodies and objective third parties. The trade media serves an important function in this regard. Often, it is useful to actually test the standards, especially when trying to implement an interoperable, standards-based solution.

I spent a year on a university task force charged with coordinating the rollout of a new campus-wide email service based on Netscape Communicator and an unspecified IMAP server. Part of our task was to determine which IMAP server to use. Unfortunately, the IMAP implementation in the early version of Communicator wasn't exactly standard. It only worked reliably with the Netscape email server. Whenever we used it with a Novonyx IMAP server, the "Inbox" would get corrupted. It has now been over a year since I left the task force, and we still haven't rolled out an IMAP email service campus-wide. A newly assembled task force is reevaluating email client and server software and will likely choose another email client.

There are a number of standards bodies that you will become familiar with as you learn more about digital convergence technologies. I've mentioned several already, and you can learn more about these organizations by visiting their respective Web sites.

Internet Engineering Task Force (IETF) at
 http://www.ietf.org
International Telecommunications Union (ITU) at
 http://www.itu.org
Motion Pictures Experts Group (MPEG) at
 http://drogo.cselt.stet.it/mpeg/
World Wide Web Consortium (W3C) at
 http://www.w3c.org

Industry Support

Industry participation in the development of a new technology (determined by the types and numbers of vendors) also says something about the evolutionary stage of that technology. Consider how industry support varies over the lifetime of an emerging technology.

■Initially, a brand new technology is most often driven by a very small number of companies. A technology start-up may be staking its future on the eventual widespread adoption of the emerging technology.

■As the technology becomes established, widespread recognition of the value and potential of the technology prompts many other start-ups and larger technology companies to join the fray.

■When the market for a new technology becomes sizable, the larger players get involved, often by buying out one or more of the original market players.

■As the technology matures, market consolidation occurs, leaving only a small number of vendors that sell and support the technology.

The influence of the very large technology providers, such as Microsoft, Intel, Cisco, and Sony, is something you should track closely. These giants have a significant impact on any emerging technology as well as the prospects for a specific product or vendor. Here's why:

(1) The entry of one of the big players will legitimize a technology, bring competition to a new level, and lead to a flurry of R&D investments and new product development. If a technology promises to fit your goals and objective, but you've been disappointed with its current performance, the participation of one of these major players may warrant another look.

(2) Once a brand new technology gains a foothold, these megaplayers may step in, using their muscle and extensive resources to attempt to take control of the technology and its market. You might want to avoid spending time and energy on a product offered by a small start-up if it appears that one of the giants may rise up and take the market away. You could be left with a product that is no longer supported if the company is driven out of business or bought.

Up to this point, I have offered a few useful ideas and insights to help you learn about technology and understand the evolution of new technologies. Now let's turn our attention to the business of deploying a specific technology.

SELECTING AND IMPLEMENTING

To successfully match a technology to your opportunities and needs, you must have a good knowledge of all relevant emerging technologies. For this reason, we've spent a great deal of time exploring this aspect of the selection process. But this process also demands that you have a solid understanding of your individual or organizational goals and objectives.

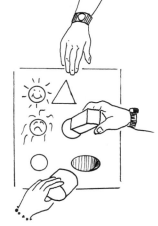

You'll be looking for a fit where a given technology appears to have a clear and significant positive impact on your ability to achieve your goals. This aspect of the matching process depends on your particular situation and your particular organization, and you must take it very seriously.

Once you've identified a potential match, you must gauge the feasibility of a prospective implementation. You'll want to fully understand any risks inherent to the technology due to its immaturity or specific technical limitations. Finally, you'll need to drill down into the details of the technology to research the costs, features, and support requirements of various products.

PRODUCT SELECTION

The selection of a particular product can be a challenging task, especially when similar technology is available from a large number of vendors. One formal, systematic approach to product selection is:

- ◆ create a comprehensive list of technical and nontechnical selection criteria (price, technical support service, etc.);
- ◆ develop a system for rating products according to those criteria; and
- ◆ apply the rating scheme to evaluate the products that might satisfy your criteria.

This approach is often used by government and corporations for complex, large-scale projects when considerable resources are at stake. The criteria are put together in a document called a request for proposal (RFP), which is then made available to vendors offering products that can meet the need. The decision makers evaluate the written proposals of vendors who have responded and select the one that best meets the need, usually within cost parameters set by management.

The RFP approach is cumbersome and time consuming. Fortunately, it is often unnecessary when implementing technology on a small scale. By identifying the factors that will be most crucial in your decision, you can quickly focus on a small number of products, possibly even getting down to a single product. For example, you may decide that you want to keep your cost to an absolute minimum; or you may require that all products must work on both Macintosh and PC computers; or you may key on a particular feature or capability. Think long and hard about these sorts of issues, and you will come up with one or two criteria that immediately narrow the field of possible products.

When I am first considering the purchase of a technology, I look closely at those characteristics and features that vary across the product offerings. You would be surprised at how quickly a few features or functions stand out as critically important. I use these functions and features as my dominant selection criteria. This simplifies product selection a great deal.

Though this approach may seem a bit like cheating, it saves considerable time and effort. Also, it ensures that you end up with a product that meets your most important criteria. The process of product selection can become a complicated project if people insist on creating exhaustive tables of criteria numerically rated for all available products. It usually isn't necessary. These folks seem never to get off the dime, as their good intentions paralyze product selection.

The Pilot

A pilot is a limited, noncritical use of a technology that is being considered for purchase. It is useful for evaluating a technology and its application, and for testing a specific product. If the technology doesn't live up to your expectations, then you have no commitments beyond the pilot. A pilot gives you a chance to get a hands-on "test drive" of how well the technology and your application will work out. The option of bailing out with minimal disruption and sunken costs is always available.

A pilot can be as simple as a one-shot limited test of a single user application, or it can be larger and more complex. An example might be a departmental pilot test of new software that you hope to eventually deploy throughout a large organization.

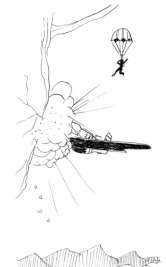

Sometimes you can get a stripped-down or demo version of the technology, reducing the cost of the pilot. Many inexpensive Internet software products allow you to download a free demo version that can be used in a pilot test.

For expensive technologies, you may need to approach vendors and ask if they are willing to give you a loaner or some sort of reduced-cost pilot. This is a good possibility if it appears to the vendor that the project may lead to significant sales down the road.

ORGANIZATIONAL CONSIDERATIONS

If you are a member of a corporate workgroup, it is important to assess the nature of your organization and its culture. In some organizations, individual and departmental innovation is encouraged and supported, and you may find it relatively easy to roll out your application on a small scale. You may even find that the organization is eager to adopt the new technology on a more widespread basis, building on your workgroup or departmental implementation.

In other organizations, the management or a central IT group may control the introduction of new technology, so you may have to work very hard to "sell" your idea before you can implement it. In this scenario, the reduced-cost pilot will be useful for demonstrating the potential value of a technology for your organization.

Even if you are working in a small organization or on your own, you need to think about the users who will be affected by the new technology. You want to design an implementation strategy that will complement the aptitude and culture of those who will be affected, so that acceptance can be achieved with as little turmoil as possible.

IMPLEMENTATION

If your pilot testing is successful, you next need to devise a plan to implement the technology on a broader, ongoing basis within your organization.

It is always advisable to pursue a gradual implementation of a new technology. One common strategy is to go from a pilot to a limited rollout of the technology to those users who have some experience and interest in using new technology. Such people are referred to as "early adopters." A variety of other techniques exists to roll out new technology incrementally, and you should be creative in considering what will work in your setting. An incremental rollout enables you to:

◆ overcome resistance to change;
◆ minimize your exposure to risks; and
◆ adapt the technology and its implementation.

It is a fact of life that many people resist the changes a new technology will require. An incremental rollout will demonstrate the benefits in a nonthreatening manner. In addition, you can react to any unforeseen problems in a timely fashion, cutting your losses early if severe, unanticipated problems arise.

You will learn a great deal as you slowly roll out a new technology, making changes where necessary to ensure the most effective end result. How you deploy and support the technology will be affected by your rollout experiences.

Your implementation plan will be affected by the complexity of the technology you want to use. System complexity will require significant technical expertise to guide the implementation, while user complexity will require in-depth training and support.

The scale of your technology deployment is another issue that will impact implementation. If you are selecting technology for yourself or your workgroup, things can be relatively straightforward and the process can move swiftly. The challenges are much greater if your plan is to implement the technology among a large group of users, such as all users on the corporate intranet. For example:

■When implementing a Web server for a small workgroup, you can easily install Web software on a desktop PC. Pages and services can be designed and tested on whatever browser is used in your workgroup, and it is likely the performance will be flawless.

■If you are implementing a Web server for tens of thousands of external Internet users, you need to ensure a secure hardware/software platform that can handle high-volume traffic with minimal downtime. You also need to design and test your pages and services on a wide variety of browsers, monitors, and modem connections to make sure they will work for a high percentage of your users. Sorting out these issues can become quite complex.

If you have never before implemented a technology service or resource, I have four recommendations for you.

Start small. Small projects are obviously more doable than large, complex projects. After the initial implementation, you can always extend the scope of the project.

Keep it simple. Explain what the technology does and how it does it in two simple sentences that anyone in your organization can understand. If you are unable to do this, your project is probably too complicated for most users, and it may very well be doomed to failure.

Be clear on costs and benefits. The benefits must be obvious and must clearly outweigh the cost of the project plus any related risks. If you aren't careful, your chances of overall success are limited, and the chance of being second-guessed is greatly increased.

Be ready to learn from failure. You are bound to have some ideas or projects that just never work out. However, a great deal can be learned from these experiences, and if you start small, the ill effects of any failure will be minimized.

As you identify and implement new technologies, keep in mind that you are building important capabilities. The technology you employ added to the expertise that you gain will provide a foundation for future technology deployments.

For example, you may decide to network the PCs in a small office so that files and printers can be shared. As you become familiar with your setup and how networks operate, it dawns on you that you can enable Internet access for your network. Consequently, the staff can more easily access information relevant to their work, and, at the same time, become electronically accessible to customers, suppliers, and colleagues. This sort of continuous building process plays out in any context, from an individual home office to a huge global corporation.

FINAL THOUGHTS

As you grapple with the activities necessary to leverage digital convergence technologies in your life and career, I'd like to leave you with some final thoughts.

ACTIVE OR PASSIVE

In Chapter 1, the link between digital convergence and human interaction was pointed out, and I have referred to it several times throughout this book. I want to explore this with you just a tiny bit further, because I believe this perspective is important as you move on to exploit new technology.

There has been a lot of talk about using digital convergence technologies for information access, especially on the Web. Certainly, that is an important aspect of digital convergence. But as new digital convergence technologies emerge, we will find that the ability of these technologies to stimulate and extend human interaction will become much more prominent. Whether you approach these new technologies as an active participant or a passive user will determine how quickly you perceive this distinction. Let's consider a couple of examples from the realm of conventional technology.

When you use the telephone, you are an active participant. Though the phone can be used to obtain information, it is primarily a tool for human interaction. On the other hand, when you watch Dan Rather on the evening news, you are a passive observer. Most likely you think of this activity as an avenue for gathering information about the day's events.

I don't know Dan Rather, but I suspect he has a different view. He knows the TV broadcast is a tool that will bring his image and voice into your living room, but he is not just concerned with the news. He knows that we are reacting not only to what he says, but also to the way it is presented. Even though Dan doesn't get our immediate feedback, he and the network do indeed get feedback in the form of mail, phone calls, email, and, ultimately, ratings. Such feedback may influence the way Dan presents himself and the news. Thus, he is an active participant, and, for him, the news broadcast is a human interaction.

As innovative individuals, entrepreneurs, and corporate workgroups are empowered to aggressively explore rich-media communication, it becomes clear that human interaction is at the center of the revolution fueled by digital convergence.

As an entrepreneur, the interaction you seek may well

take the form of a financial transaction. You present information about your products or services on a Web site, and visitors to your site may decide to respond with an online purchase. Much depends on how greatly your Web-site visitors need the product or service, and how well you make your presentation.

In the sphere of higher education, a great deal of attention focuses on technology-enabled human interaction for new distance-learning courses. This method of teaching includes a mix of technology-based synchronous and asynchronous human interactions. Videoconferencing, discussion forums, email, and the Web are now commonly used to support teaching and learning. However, technology-based human interaction is not limited to courses of instruction.

I subscribe to a listserv where academics exchange ideas on the use of technology in higher education. Until recently, this listserv had been a text-based email discussion. The moderator of the list, Steve Gilbert, decided to put together a Real Media stream consisting of a narrated slide show on the impact and issues of technology deployment in higher ed. He sent out the Web address of this multimedia experience to the listserv along with an invitation to send him feedback.

I checked it out, and it was really quite well done. However, I felt that his presentation focused on accessing information and how overwhelming that task can be for academics, but it failed to explore the capability of new technology to facilitate human interaction. Therefore, I decided to put together a video stream of my own to congratulate Steve on breaking through the text barrier and to comment on the importance of human interaction versus information access.

Steve posted my message on the listserv with an embedded video link. Over 6,500 professors, university administrators, and technology professionals and instructors subscribe to this listserv, and my message created a bit of a stir. I received email from all over the world. Of course, there were a few dissenters, but most people could see my point. I believe this was a useful human interaction between me and the hundreds or thousands of people who took the time to view the video.

When pursuing new technology, contemplate its power to bring people together. Consider customer service, distance learning, or any number of areas where there is a real opportunity to make a difference with new technology. The spoon that stirs the pot in these applications is human interaction, not information access.

HERE'S TO THE LITTLE GUY

My closing thought also revisits a theme you've seen throughout this book: the ability of digital convergence technologies to empower the entrepreneur, individual, or corporate workgroup. This is a revolution in which the little guy is actively shaping the application of new technology.

"How did they do that?" or "Why did they do that?" are phrases I've heard since I was a kid. The "they" in these sentences are usually distant, powerful corporate entities. Throughout my lifetime, "they" have done a whole bunch of things that are pretty amazing. "They" gave us the new Corvette, toll-free telephone numbers, sneakers with lights in the heels, and *Seinfeld.* When I was growing up, I hoped that I would some day get a job with "them" as a little cog in a big wheel.

Emerging digital convergence technologies enable a new paradigm for getting ahead. This technology offers each of us an opportunity to become "them" in some small way.

The Web has demonstrated how digital convergence technologies level the playing field. The Web is empowering, but most Web sites are still limited to text and graphics. Streaming media enables us to move into rich-media presentations and interactions, and it is a technology that actually presents the little guy with an advantage. In fact, streaming media is near the top of my list of rapidly maturing digital convergence technologies that have the potential to significantly impact how we learn, work, and play.

Streaming media, out of the box, is a useful and powerful technology for the individual entrepreneur or corporate workgroup. However, streaming media does not scale well for large numbers of users. The huge spikes in demand that mass audiences generate dramatically increase the complexity of deploying this Internet tool. From the point of view of broadcasters, it's not particularly useful. Yet it continues to divert eyeballs away from conventional broadcasts.

If my small start-up company wants to deliver a compelling and powerful experience via the Internet, it can be done with simple, straightforward, and reliable low-scale streaming-media technology. The media can be delivered live or in on-demand mode, and there's no need to worry about multicasting or stream propagation. I could be quite pleased to reach a micro-niche audience. Though the income stream generated is modest compared to what a larger corporation expects, the small audience can deliver significant dollars to my company. This is especially true because my electronic delivery costs are so low and I've cut out the middleman.

These are the seeds of a competitive advantage for me, the little guy. Also reinforced is the notion that digital convergence is a powerful force for empowering individuals and workgroups via one-to-one and one-to-few human interactions. It is not just a platform for big corporations to increase market share with mass products, services, and media.

I've had streaming media available through my personal

Web site for some time, and it works great. I'll be putting up streaming media at *http://www.digital-convergence.com* after finishing this book. Because I expect a relatively modest-sized audience, I won't need to worry about swamping the Internet with video streams. I won't have to mess with scheduled multicast programming, and I can use a video server that is based on a standard desktop PC. Come see for yourself how well it works.

The larger players counter the little guy's advantage by throwing considerable resources at streaming media development and related functions to up the ante on quality and functionality. This strategy is frequently seen on the Web sites of large corporations and media companies, where well-paid media professionals are hired to push the envelope on high-end technology.

Still, I get excited when I see how digital convergence seems to favor the individual or small-time entrepreneur. Many talented people are out there who will craft wonderfully creative services and resources with this new technology. I hope you are one of them.

INDEX